Tom McCahill

Today's Sports and Competition Cars

Tom McCahill

Today's Sports and Competition Cars

PRENTICE-HALL, INC.
Englewood Cliffs, N.J.

To the Internal Revenue Service. Without their constant prodding and urging, this book would never have been written. If enough copies are sold, perhaps they'll leave me a crumb or two.

Library of Congress Catalog Card No.: 59-8030

Printed in the United States of America

92473

Contents

1

Today's Competition Car

COMPETITION CARS COME IN AS MANY SHAPES and sizes as girls do, and for just about as many different purposes. It takes no talent whatsoever to start an Irish saloon brawl among the advocates of the various types of competition cars. The sports car man thinks the speed trial booster is an adolescent neophyte, and the rally man watching a friend bend and break a sports car in a hard race feels the driver is a meatball for the Anglo-Italian-Stuttgart parts houses.

Back in 1954, when I wrote *The Modern Sports Car,* the picture was entirely different. Available automobiles for the most part consisted of Detroit iron mines, sports cars and Grand Prix cars. Nothing coming out of Detroit was worth a second look by the competition man, and the small imports of the day had little, if any, appeal to the non-truss-users. The picture has changed considerably since then, and there are now more connoisseurs around than you could jam in the state of Alaska with modern baling equipment.

Shortly after World War II, the writer invented the phrase "Detroit Iron"—which aptly described the domestic output until well after the mid-century. Postwar cars coming from the state of Michigan had less to recommend them than an oboe solo at a missile launching. But when Detroit cars started getting factory backing in competition, weird things emerged from their stamping plants. These things were some automobiles that were truly great.

Now the professional sports car snob will still wince at anything with a Detroit label, but this can be put down, in many cases, as a gesture of self-conscious ignorance. It's quite a simple matter to prove this to you, a member of the intelligentsia, and, since you've bothered to buy (or steal) this book, here it is: As you undoubtedly know, the hard core of imported-car fanciers are, like the hard core of any other over-enthusiastic group, hard to convince; but then there are seven other sides to a square. The basic difference between most imports and American cars of similar price range today is that, on the imports, the quality of material and workmanship is much finer, even to an untrained eye. But there are other factors, including engineering, that are often strong enough to offset quality advantages.

I did say I'd give you proof, so here it is: Take some of the better-endowed-than-average sports car and import enthusiasts and leaf through their car stables to find out what they drive. This should prove a fairly convincing argument to the one-or-two-car Deutschland- and Brittanica-forever nuts. Let's start off with Briggs Cunningham, who has done more to foster sports cars in America than any other three men combined. Briggs owns better than 50 of the finest imports, ranging from

Bentleys and Ferraris to Lister Jags and other Jaguars (he is the importer of Jaguar cars in the East). For his go-to-work-and-knock-around car does he use one of his old Cunninghams? He might—but nine times out of ten you'll find him driving his Chrysler 300 or Imperial.

Bill Spear, former Cunningham team driver and the owner of many imports from Oscas to Bentley Continentals, teamed up with Sherwood Johnston (also a LeMans driver and Ferrari owner) to win the Berkshire Rally—what in? A Chrysler Imperial. The cost-is-no-object big-timers in the sports car field drive American cars just as often as they do imports. Some creep once said, "There's a place for everything, and everything in its place," and some American cars have earned a very definite niche in automobile prestige.

This is not a slam against sports cars—which are fun to own and drive—but an attempt at true evaluation for today. Some American cars, with little or no reworking, can give some of the greatest sports cars a real pushing on courses that are considered sports car courses alone. For instance, let's consider the new Bridgehampton Race Course located on Long Island. The first big race held there was won by a competition Lister-Jaguar, expertly driven by Walt Hansgen at an average speed of 82.5 mph. A few weeks later a late model stock car race was held over the same course—a course specially built for sports car racing. The winning stock Chevrolet averaged 81.5—just one mph short of the Lister-Jaguar. There is room for all types of competition cars, including some Americans, so before tossing those brickbats, it might not be a bad idea to examine some of their facets.

Perhaps the biggest enemy of the American car, to the true automobile man, is the Madison Avenue Ad Kid. Navel-deep in superlatives, innuendos and exaggerations, he loads the public with false and non-existent claims to fame. Actually, Detroit engineers have proven to this writer's satisfaction that they can make a fairly passable bird, but they don't know how to teach it to fly. When the Detroit factories started getting into heavy competition on the race tracks of the country, the various engineering departments were not only astounded, but fairly well miffed by the fact that outsiders (in many cases without even a high school degree) could make their automobiles run ten to twenty per cent better and faster than the factories themselves could.

This was a bitter pill for the younger engineers to swallow, but swallow it they did, because they were getting their brains beaten out by the competition who were hiring garage mechanics, hillbillies and even moonshiners who knew a thing or two never found in textbooks on how to get a few more twirls out of a standard factory engine. Race mechanics were rounded up like spilt pearls on a ballroom floor. Chevrolet hired Smoky Yunick, an ex-bomber-jockey who ran a speed shop in Daytona Beach. Ford latched on to Red Vogt of Atlanta. Plymouth called in Bill Frick of Long Island. Lincoln-Mercury grabbed on to the late Clay Smith and his partner, Bill Stroppe. Others who answered the call were race driver Mauri Rose to Chevy, Arkus-Duntov to Corvette, Pete DePaolo to Ford, and, before the other manufacturers got into the act, the late Marshall Teague, a Daytona Beach gas station operator, made the Hudson factory cars win for years. American cars, *some* of them, have come a long ways since we verbally ripped them apart in *The Modern Sports Car* back in '54.

With the increased popularity of racing, dozens of new tracks have been built throughout the land. Actual road racing, which was still popular in 1954, has all but vanished in this country, and in its place has come racing on specially built courses. Not all of these were good and only a few have made money, because, as Austy Clark, a big shareholder in the Bridgehampton layout, pointed out to the writer, the typical sports car competitor is a pretty lousy showman. He went on to say, "It's hard to interest a crowd in spending money to watch a group of junior advertising executives give it a go on a warm Saturday afternoon." A hassle has gone on for years between amateur and professional sports car driving, which was hardly calculated to tickle the fancies of the ticket-buying public. When a man pays to see a sports event, he wants to see the real thing, not just a reasonable facsimile.

Some of the better courses at this writing are Bridgehampton, Elkhart Lake, and Daytona Beach, where the new 2½ mile track, the fastest in the country, has a built-inside sports car road course. This is the biggest and best track built in America since Indianapolis was laid down almost a half century ago.

Sports cars have undergone a change in the last five years that can hardly be listed as an improvement if you happen to be a stickler for the original conception of what a sports car is. Actually, no man ever succeeded in accurately defining what a sports car is, morally, and the FIA (Fédération International de l'Automobile) laid down a set of rules which contains more loopholes than a boxcar loaded with Cheerios. Generally, it was conceded that a sports car was a general-purpose ambidextrous vehicle that could be used for hustling groceries from the store, hauling a girlfriend to Lover's Lane, and racing on Saturdays or Sundays. It was a car you'd take on your annual trip to Florida or the Coast, or enter in a race at Bridgehampton or Watkins Glen. Ten years ago the MG filled this bill perfectly, as a quality little bucket, fun to drive and even more fun to race.

Today, due to rule chiseling and tradition-raping,

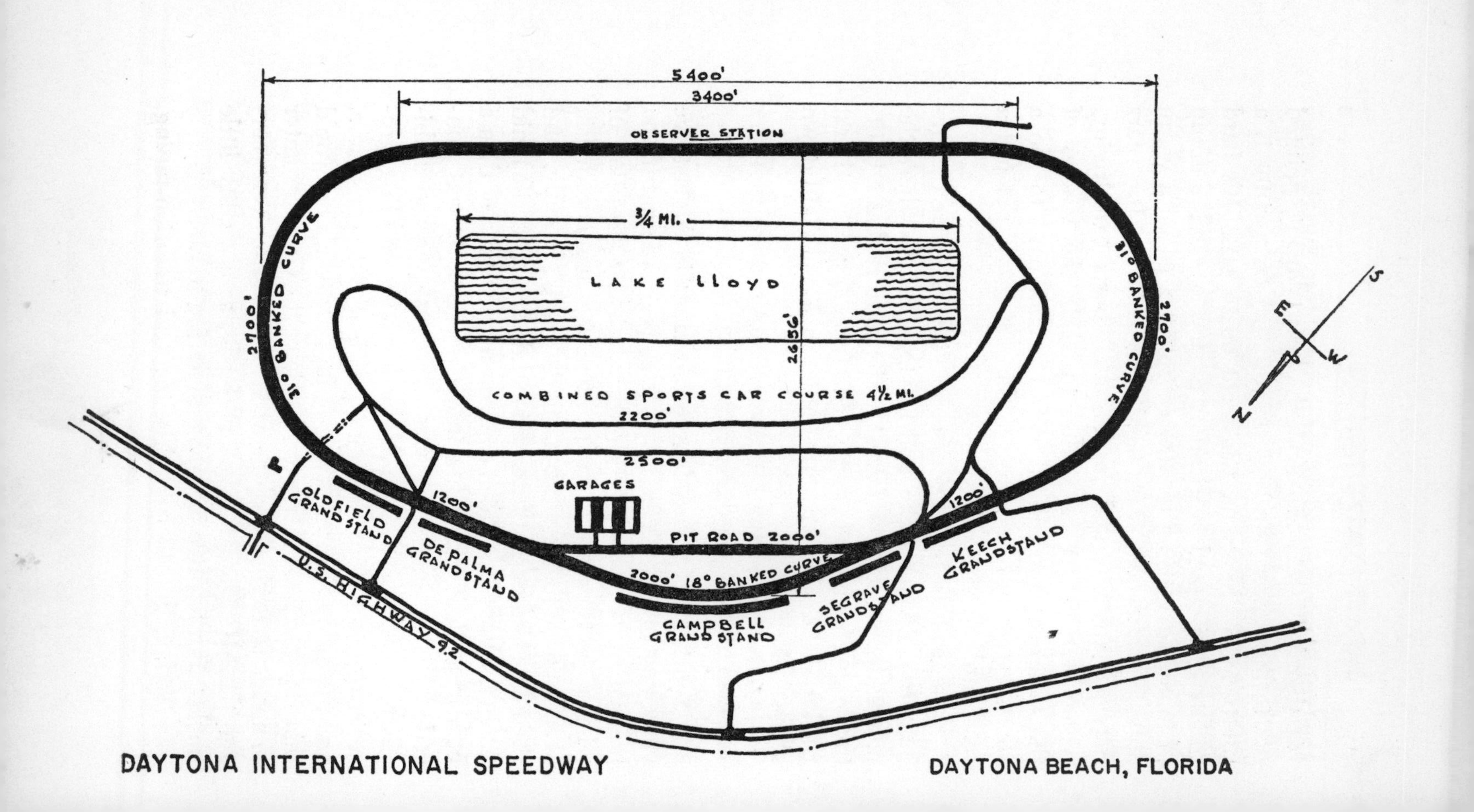

DAYTONA INTERNATIONAL SPEEDWAY

DAYTONA BEACH, FLORIDA

the typical winning sports car is one of two things: either an out-and-out race car or an out-and-out fraud. For anyone intelligent enough to explore the contents of a beer can, with cars like the Lister Jag, D-Jag, Lotus, Scarab, Osca, Elva and many others of this ilk, using the nomenclature "sports car" instead of "race car" is like dubbing Juliet an "overworked harlot."

Ninety-nine per cent of the serious competitors at sports car races today are towed there either on trailers or in vans. Just a few short years ago all the contestants at LeMans arrived and departed under their own power, except those who were no longer capable of doing so. Many old-timers remember the first resurrection of the Bridgehampton race back in '49 when all the sports cars raced were driven there with spare parts aboard, and in some cases, with wives and children—and that's the way they left. That was sports car racing in the true tradition. Today, many a young executive wraps himself in a race car cockpit on Saturdays, exchanging his horn rims for prescription goggles, and plays *man*. Good sports, no doubt, but bad theatre.

The sports cars of the early 1950's that could be used for everything, including a honeymoon or taking a dog to the vet's, are still with us in more modern form. Such cars as the Austin Healey, Porsche, Triumph, Morgan, MG, and quite a few others are still able to fill the sports car bill as it was originally thought of, as all-purpose fun cars. For the most part, though, these are now considered by the pointed-head set as touring cars. Touring cars they are, but also sports cars.

In 1954, we warned that when LeMans first allowed alcohol fuel to be used in 1953, replacing that old staid pump fuel, there was a definite danger to sports cars as we knew them. As builders explored the chiseling possibilities in the F.I.A. sports car definitions, it soon became apparent that all a sports car had to be to meet the rules was a Grand Prix race car just slightly stretched in the cockpit to call it a "two-seater"—though no two normal-sized 15-year-old boys could sit in it at the same time. They had to cut in a door (which was farcical in proportions) and the car usually had to have a lighting system. Any sharp Italian tinsmith with a good pair of snippers could accomplish the necessary alterations to work a Grand Prix race car into a "sports car" before the dew had dried in the olive patch.

Another kind of competition car which we'll discuss further in this book and which has really shot up in popularity in the last few years is the rally car. It can vary in size from the Monte-Carlo rally-winning Dauphine to the American rally-winning Imperial; but most popular in this class are the small, gutty imports with fantastic roadability that can be maneuvered through a crowded hall closet. They are more fun to drive, for a real driver, because through real driving there is more to get out of them than the average duffer can cope with. Cars such as the Swedish-built Saabs and Volvos are fantastic road cars for assaulting snowy mountains or serpentine back roads. At the same time they are good family cars for general use and, in my book, the owner of one of these is every bit as much of a sports car man as the owner of a Ferrari.

Rallies have become the major automotive sport in the country today, which isn't at all surprising, since they allow the whole family to participate, the cars are seldom harmed, and a victory proves not only that the man behind the wheel is a top driver, but that he had a navigator who knew which end was up. Though it doesn't take as much guts as broadsliding into a corner at 100 mph-plus, it often calls for as much skill to maintain a perfect average over unknown winding roads.

Racing reached a danger point a few years ago. Too much horsepower tied up with too little ability has caused many tragedies that have tended to give racing a black eye. You old-timers among the sports car fraternity may recall that post-war sports car racing progressed for several years before there was a single fatality, despite many races. Then more and more new drivers entered the sport, and cars began to get faster and faster. The writer pointed out then that this was a combination that spelled disaster in capital letters. As soon as businessmen started racing at Mercedes and Ferrari team speeds on weekends, the die was cast—many would be killed.

For years in Europe, team drivers for Mercedes, Auto-Union, Alfa-Romeo and other big camps had a six-day week, even in off-seasons. Day after day, these men would put in hundreds of miles of practice driving. Trained like athletes, they knew exactly to the thousandth just how far their steeds could be pushed, and just how far they couldn't. What's more important, they knew what to do if they goofed and found themselves crossed up. Despite this, many of the best were killed, which was to be expected, since professionals were racing against other professionals and all pushed their talents to the breaking point. These fellows were entirely different from many of the sports car drivers who have been killed on these shores in recent years. There's a long, long jump between an 85 mph MG and a 170 mph competition Jag—but many unprofessional enthusiasts made the jump. Some got away with it and some didn't.

A typical example may be Hypothetical P. Boyd. A car fan for years, he has driven to Florida several times from New York. He spends five days a week as sales manager for a big corporation. He lunches at "21" every noon, and meets the boys at the Harvard Club for martinis before taxiing home for more martinis at his home on East 72nd Street. The usual mixed bag of dinner parties and occasional theatre fills out his otherwise dull week. His big love is his 250 hp racing sports car, which he keeps at Alberghetti Moosepops famed garage. On race weekends he checks out of the office early on Friday, drives to the course for some practice runs, a few martinis, dinner, and so to bed.

He rises early on Saturday morning, since he's entered in the feature event. Moosepop and his boys, in shiny flameproof coveralls, greet the master in the pit area as he strolls to his mount. This picture is more typical than not. Later in the afternoon, when our hero finds one or two of the semi-pros crowding him in a hard bend, he may, if he's intelligent enough, suddenly realize and say to himself, "What the hell am I doing in this company? These guys are out to kill me. I'm a sales manager —not a professional race driver." If he does just that, he may back off and live. However, if he decides to give it that good old school try, he may wind up at the pearly gates on the first bounce. Quite a few have.

This chapter is on competition cars, but I'd like to go on record and state that the Saturday afternoon driver who feels he can match wheelturn for wheelturn with the semi-pro is nine times out of ten an undiluted lunatic. Sports cars capable of doing 150 mph should be driven only by pros, or by amateurs with little if anything else to do. Men who have to work five days a week and who drive less than 25,000 miles a year should stick to the slower-class cars, because the muscle toning and timing needed to drive the faster rigs just isn't available to the occasional driver when he must have it. Fast driving, like golf, tennis, or any other sport, should only be attempted by those in top condition—you can't possibly work five days a week at something other than automobiles and be an expert big car driver on weekends; just as a weekend golfer can't expect to shoot par with the consistency of the pro who plays every day. The only difference is that in golf no one gets killed. When the weekend Fangio goofs, usually several other souls are around to join him on his trip to Paradise—often some really top-notch drivers who couldn't get out of the way in time.

I have a fairly large living room in my home. If I could throw a cocktail party for all the men I've known personally who have been killed racing in the last five years, I couldn't jam them into the house, all standing up. Among this group would be quite a few pros, and quite a few amateurs who were killed, in most cases, because they were driving way over their heads and far beyond their talents. A professional is usually paid well to take chances, but an amateur who does it for nothing is an idiot. In the old days, before the first post-World War II sports car driver was killed, I'm sure the drivers had as much fun in slower, less potent vehicles. Though the skill level demanded was not as high, the "jollies" were still there, as they say in Hollywood. If you want to race, and you're going to race, my advice is to do it in a car that matches your talent. Many a guy who has looked like an awful white-livered stroker in his Ferrari might have been a king in a Triumph.

Sports cars? Rally cars? Speed trials cars? They can all be fun, if approached at the proper level. The pride that you'll get from a well-won race in a sports car can also be enjoyed by the man and his navigator who take a big-time rally, and if you don't think the fellow who has tuned his car to a point where it'll outrun several hundred other cars in a big-time speed trial such as at Daytona Beach every February, gets a thrill, then you've never tried it.

2

Who Buys Sports Cars?

FIVE KINDS OF PEOPLE BUY SPORTS CARS—THE Competitor, the Prestige Seeker, the Mechanical Snob, the Exhibitionist, and the Connoisseur. The current sports car popularity phenomenon is both a natural part of the changing American way of life since World War II and the return of a very old American tradition. Sports cars are as *un*-Communistic as a $350.00 custom-made suit, or a $3,000 brace of Purdey shotguns. Sports cars are American as apple pie and the Fourth of July—as a way of life.

Examining the picture closely, it's pretty obvious that the United States, more than any other country, should be sports car minded. This is a nation made up largely of people who resent regimentation and personal-habit dictatorship. For generations Americans have proven that they are individuals, with individual thoughts. They are at their best when they're prosperous, not only as individuals but as independent, creative operators. Most sports cars are different in the extreme from the commonplace products of Michigan, and there are enough models and makes available to give the American buyer a nonregimented, uncommon-man feeling. The average American, regardless of whether he plays baseball, a hot fiddle, or dollar-a-point Gin, aspires from the day of birth to be better than just a common man. The more successful he becomes, the harder he will strive for individualism. Many such men have resented owning cars that looked just like everyone else's. Aside from his home, his automobile is quite often a man's largest investment, and quite rightly he may feel that this should have features and looks unlike the average flotsam and jetsam.

The sports car, with its intriguing lines, and un-run-of-the-mill performance, is filling the gap for a lot of owners demanding something *different* and more exclusive than a chrome-trimmed steel stamping produced by the millions. Through its very un-bus-like capacity and limited space, it has become classified as a luxury product. Many of these cars are not to be owned by a man with a family of more than two, or by a man with bulky hauling chores. By reason of their very size, sports cars become as practical as a Hattie Carnegie evening gown for doing housework, or a mink coat for sweeping out a barn, in the average one-car family-man's scheme of life. The one-car, low-income breadwinner will find justifying a sports car an almost impossible thing to do, unless he is that paragon of manly virtues who successfully refuses to allow his wife to drive and always leaves the kids home. Sports cars are only for the family man with a fairly sizable bank account—that is, if he likes to take the kiddies along.

The Competitor

Sports car speeds range from the comparatively slow 95 mph of the MG to better than 190 mph with some hotter cars. But a lot more than performance has caused the present tremendous popularity of the different types of sports cars. The competition owner, the man who bought the car to race, is in the very small minority. But in the past five years, road-type racing has become a major spectator sport and hardly a month goes by that several large events are not held in states ranging from coast to coast and Maine to Texas. These amateur drivers range from the single-MG owner-driver to several individuals who own teams that race not only in the United States, but in Europe during the season. Some of these endeavors represent huge personal expenditures. Like professional golfers on the tournament circuit, the race men cover the 48 states competing, but these competitors number less than 1,000, only a drop in the bucket compared to the thousands of sports cars now being sold in every state.

The Prestige Seeker

More than 80 per cent of all sports cars are owned by people with no intention of ever competing in a contest involving speed. Perhaps the most frequent buyer of sports cars is the Prestige Seeker, just as it was many years ago in the 20's. These owners, either men or women, are quite often the ones you will find attending the opening night at the opera, or in Scotland on August 12th, at the opening of the grouse season. They like everything they own to be the best but, most important of all, they insist that it be different. Prestige owners, like any other group, come in a variety of pocketbook sizes and idiosyncrasies. Not all can afford Scotland's grouse shooting, or even the jewel equipment needed for the first night at the Met, but they pursue their individuality as far as their means will allow and seek exclusiveness within their price ranges.

Just as it was 30 years ago, possibly the largest group of prestige owners will be found in the theatrical world and its offshoots, television, radio, etc. Unfortunately, due to economic pressures, it has not always been possible for the American people to be rugged individualists and to avoid the unglamorous pitfalls often brought on by production-line living. The current increased sales of foreign cars is not merely the carrying-on of a tradition that died with the depression, and remained dead through World War II. Thirty or more years ago, before the depression, movie stars of the day, and other notable personalities, vied for attention with huge mansions, Scott Fitzgerald parties, and, always, automobiles.

In the 1920's there were very few of what could be called "sports cars" around, but there were exhibition pieces that in some cases resembled miniature Taj Mahals on wheels (and ten times the number of car manufacturers in this country than there are today). No one who was anyone would have been found dead in a Cadillac, or similar car, in those days, and the celebrity who didn't boast at least three $20,000-plus, four-wheeled imports, or American greats, was practically in a personal depression. In New York, Mayor Jimmy Walker had a $25,000 Duesenberg limousine for his go-to-work car. Mary Pickford preferred the Hispano-Suiza, and Douglas Fairbanks for years stuck to the big Fiat, when it resembled a locomotive. Rudolph Valentino had an Isotta-Fraschini with a huge cobra radiator ornament, as did Peggy Joyce and Harry Richman. Vincent Youmans, whose "Tea for Two" we still dance to, had a racing Mercedes for daytime use and a Rolls-Royce limousine for evenings at the theater. Many tycoons, like J. C. Penny, stuck to the glamorous sleeve-valve Minerva from Belgium, and the real sporty ones, like Edsel Ford and Briggs S. Cunningham, drove Mercedes with out-of-the-hood exhaust pipes and a roar that would shake the countryside for miles around.

Detroit's production lines were operating every day, just as now, building cars by the thousands, but these were more or less for the plebeian buyers, certainly not for the wealthy sportsmen who on an African safari demanded that the beaters be Yale men. Mercers, Stutz and even the big Packard 8 Phaeton, with huge drum spotlights mounted on running board stanchions, were passable American equipment and in no way related to the usual family hack. Today Hollywood has gone back to the Rolls-Royce as a symbol of success.

The prestige cars of these early days were gargantuan monsters, many of them weighing more than three tons. They were representative of an era that died like a well-drilled dove back on that October day in '29. After the depression, which lasted more than ten years, we found ourselves in World War II, which lasted another four. During this entire period, some fifteen years, nothing could have seemed less important, as a whole, than owning a glamour barge. Most of the companies that made these former eye-catchers went out of business. In early 1946, when new production cars were again rolling off the Detroit lines, a car-starved country was only too glad to accept warmed-over versions of the prewar family sedan. In fact, thousands of people paid large under-the-counter bonuses just to get them. As drab as this picture was, there was nothing else to buy.

However, fortunes had been made during the war and there was a new crop of celebrities waiting for something different. In 1948 the TC MG, a little car the size of a child's pony, caught the eye of many already bored with commonplace, dull Detroit transportation. By 1950 hardly a star in Hollywood with enough influence to talk back occasionally to a director, could be found who did not own one of these little jewel-like bugs. Hundreds of young men back from the wars, many of them fighter pilots like John Fitch, who shot down the first jet plane in combat, were not ready to settle for golf and hot sessions of Canasta in the evening. The boys stationed in Europe sopped up much of the lore of road racing, a major sport over there, and by June of 1949, under the auspices of the newly formed Sports Car Club of America, this group held its first big-time race at Bridgehampton, Long Island, where these races had been a feature 30 years before, as an offshoot of the Vanderbilt Cup days.

Overnight, this racing glamour caught on like wildfire, and more and more imports were brought over, spark-plugged by Briggs Cunningham who introduced the first Ferrari to this country, and went on to build his own sports cars. The prestige buyers of old—the Hollywood stars, the new TV performers, and the still-uncelebrated World War II millionaires, plus a number of the old-time buyers dating back to the 20's—weren't getting the glamour cars of more than twenty years before. There were no Isotta-Fraschinis, as long as canal barges, or gold-trimmed Hispanos.

Prestige buyers were becoming bored by Cadillacs, Lincolns, and Packards, which everyone owned, when along came this upstart—the sports car with its classic or streamlined design, depending upon make, packaged in a variety of colors and with lush appointments. The prestige buyers went for them like a starving man stumbling onto a steak. Today, just as 30 years ago, there's hardly a top name in show business, or any other form of gilded endeavor, who hasn't one or two foreign sports cars in his garage.

By 1954 foreign sports cars were being used more and more in fashion ads, or by beer and whiskey companies, as backgrounds displaying clothes or a cooling glass of suds. Even American oil companies and spark plug manufacturers lean heavily on these sports cars for background and glamour. Large advertising companies, even some with huge Detroit accounts, quickly recognized the glamour appeal of sports cars in their advertising of other products. The prestige buyer once again became exclusive and in nearly any country club, or fancier bar, volumetric efficiency and horsepower per liter were discussed with all the enthusiasm usually accorded the World Series results on the sawdust circuit of Third Avenue. Listen to any disc-jockey long enough and he'll get in a plug for his Austin-Healey or Porsche.

The Mechanical Snob

Now to another type of buyer, the Mechanical Snob, who for all practical purposes, is a rather disagreeable individual, firmly believing that anything built this side of Greenland is a totally impossible mess. These fellows are usually jam packed with misinformation and can spout long technical terms (which few of them can understand) by the hour. They can recite the volumetric efficiency of the 1930 Bentley faster than Two-Horse Harry can give you the complete blood line of last year's Preakness winner. They can spend hours discussing the merits of the centrifugal blower, or the advantages of the five-speed gear box. They are usually dressed in the latest non-pressed English tweeds and can tell you to the second the correct saddle soap to use on the adjustment straps in the backs of their short-peak caps.

To them this is a very solemn business and no levity is allowed to enter their conversations about what they refer to as "Motor Cars." They know America is in the hands of hopeless barbarians from Detroit, and to them the man who has just bought a Cadillac is a lost soul.

Fortunately, this group is very small, but, just as unfortunately, they have a way of making their presence known like a thousand voices from atop a soapbox. Unlike the prestige buyer, who buys the sports car for fun and for pride of possession, the Mechanical Snob can be happy living out his entire life with an early TC MG that looks as though it has been standing under Niagara Falls for twelve years.

The Exhibitionist

Another type of owner is the Exhibitionist. This character usually guts his mufflers so that everyone will hear him, wears the loudest clothes, talks the loudest and squeals his tires, even when driving into his own garage. This buyer is a good friend of Detroit, for when he turns up in a sports car he makes Detroit products look virtuous indeed.

The Connoisseur

Our last type of owner is the real Connoisseur. This man *knows* automobiles and can appreciate what the sports car can do for him. He understands the suspension, the engine, and every other part of his sports car. He knows how to drive it well and is often, though not necessarily, a competition man. This man enjoys being well mounted and gets his kick out of knowing he is driving the best in four-wheeled transportation. If he has the money and needs a truck or a bus for hauling his family he'll buy an American station wagon, or sedan, in addition to a sports car. He won't sneer at the American car—these are good utilitarian work horses to him, the best in the world for what they do, but for his personal pleasure he'll stick to the sports car. This is the doll he uses for commuting, or for that trip to the Coast, if that's where his business takes him.

The Connoisseur usually looks on his sports car as a sporting companion, not just a piece of steel, some iron and some rubber. To him the sports car is a friend, something to be admired, appreciated and treated with respect. It is the pinnacle of the mechanical engineer's art. No successful sports car in the world was ever built with a fast buck in mind. No sports car designer ever built a car just to please the bottom of some plush dowager. He built a car for adventure, performance, and all the thrill a good road can give a good driver in a good vehicle. The Connoisseur considers the sports car to be the epitome of Machine Age culture.

Rolled into a tight ball, the sports car story, more or less, adds up as follows: They have brought to these shores a new type of racing sport practically unknown to Americans not old enough to remember the Vanderbilt Cup days. They have given the prestige buyer a new replacement for the three-ton juggernaut of the 20's with an extra dash that the cars of the 20's never had. The sports car has the pride-of-possession appeal, rarely found in today's stamped industrial products. It is a great conversation piece and an eyecatcher, but most of all it has brought fun back to the highway. Many a businessman who five years ago commuted to work in a family sedan, counting off the moments until his arteries froze, now whips through the same chore, top down, rosy cheeked and with a wandering eye for the girls. The sports car has blown life into many an over-the-hill executive. It's another shot at youth and adventure. If you are a sports car owner you know what I mean. If you're not, hurry up —it's not as late as you think.

3

How About A Sports Car?

As I was about to start writing this chapter, I received a phone call from an editorial writer on a New York paper. Though I had never met the caller, he opened the conversation like this: "Hey, McCahill, they tell me you know all about sports cars, and I've read some of your books, so would you please tell me what the hell is a sports car?"

"Damned if I know," I believe I told him (which was the truth), and it is my sincere belief that, aside from the sticky F.I.A. formula, no one has ever accurately defined to everyone's satisfaction just what a sports car is. It is my belief that a sports car is more a state of mind than anything else, with one or two factors to hang a hook onto. The oldest definition of a sports car, and perhaps the truest, is that it is a competition vehicle with utilitarian properties, or vice versa. In other words, a vehicle being labeled a sports car by the manufacturers is one step (except when Detroit does it). Another step is your buying the car with an occasional, or many, races in mind, and at the time of purchase realizing it must be your business car and general errand hack. Or, to put it a 27th way, the general state of mind known as a sports car by most sports car men is a car in which you can woo your gal, pick up a case of scotch, or, with a few slight adjustments, race at Bridgehampton, Watkins Glen or any other suitable course.

The fact you can race it with a reasonable chance of winning, even if only a class win, makes the car a sports car to just about everybody's satisfaction. The only fly in the ointment is that a guy can buy a hot Detroit bomb with the same purpose in mind and race it on the late-model stock car circuit, if he cares to. So, as you can see, we're right up in the air again with that guy in the Chinese balloon.

My idea of a sports car, though I definitely couldn't make it stick in court, is an automobile that is basically a piece of sporting equipment. A piece of equipment that had sport more in mind when it was being designed than yanking Madame Suburbia to the A & P. Like a fine shotgun that is designed for ducks at Currituck or live pigeon tournaments in Portugal; in other words, a piece of sporting equipment. Though you could shoot ducks at Currituck and possibly win money at live pigeons in Portugal with an ugly Sing Sing riot gun, it would hardly make the riot gun a "Sportsman's Fowling Piece" except to an underprivileged mind.

My type of sports car is a beautifully executed, athletic machine that corners like oil through a pipe, has a reasonably high degree of performance and an overall finish and appearance that strikes the nicety core in your brain cells—something fine, like a piece of Revere silver or a Cellini vase. A good sports car, like any other piece of good sporting equipment, should be something you can work up a real affection for. You may even have a pet name for it, and you may even talk to it, when you're alone, because you and the sports car, out on the road, are a couple of pals together, and if you're incapable of working up such affection over a jewel-like piece of machinery, you'd be far better off with a Buick.

My type of sports car, whether it's small and comparatively slow or big and gutty, must have one thing, and that is quality. The upholstery must be the finest; the bodywork must reflect craftsmanship, and not the best that could be turned out on a flat-rate schedule; and the engineroom must be clean, functional and uncluttered with tripe. It must be a car I'd be proud to drive; in fact, so proud I could genuinely and wholeheartedly laugh in the face of the man with the El Dorado Brougham. A sports car is basically for a sportsman, and exhibitionists who buy them for show, but without feeling, actually detract from all sports cars. Sports cars are an acquired taste, and are rarely fully appreciated except by buyers who are either sportsmen basically or just desire the better things in life.

Whether a sports car is, in your scheme of things, an only or a second car, you alone can say. There are many sports cars of many types available, but from a practical standpoint, and especially for the man with non-competition intent, only a few of these are generally popular enough to assure nationwide service. A buyer in the vicinity of a big metropolitan area like New York or Los Angeles can find service for anything from a split french horn to a moth-ridden toupee. In other sections, however, rarer imports could easily prove as practical as a Jimmy Walker courtesy card to a current West Side cop.

Many imports are now so common that they're easier

to get serviced than several makes of American cars. However, for the buyer who demands exclusiveness in his product, for bowling over the awe-struck peasants, cars such as the Corvette, Jag, MG and Triumph may easily be too common. There are other cars available with the sexy exclusiveness of five eyes that can still be rated as serviceable transportation—not total mysteries at any up-to-date sports car salon. The following is a list of sports cars that not only are easy to buy, but also should be fairly easy to have serviced in most of the English-speaking sections of our country. And we'll drop one or two in that are calculated to keep them guessing for an hour or so.

MG

The MG is the little stinker that started the post-World War II boom in sports cars, with its famous spider-wheeled TC. In their day they could trim anything Detroit produced in a coast-to-coast run, because they managed to stay on the road even when it varied from straight. The MG, for reasons that will remain forever unknown to this writer, rested on the McKinley ticket too long. When the TD was introduced to take the TC's place, it was hardly a step forward—the TD was uglier and not one bit faster than the TC, and, though these cars only displaced 1¼ liters, they were forced to race in the 1½-liter class. This ridiculous unneeded handicap made the TD owner who desired some competition a thorough meatball. It would be like trying to fight Dempsey in his prime while wearing snowshoes.

After the TD came the Mark II which was a hopped-up version that still stood at 1¼-liters, for reasons best known to Lord Nuffield and his Brownies. The MG was built like an aircraft carrier, and actually had larger, heavier frames than Cadillacs of the day, so they spotted everything to the competition, aside from smallpox and epilepsy. The MG owners, which included the writer, were loyal—but loyalty can never override stupidity. When hot 1½-liter cars such as the Osca and Porsche made their appearances, to win a one and a half liter race in an MG became as easy as it would be for Roy Rogers to beat a jet liner on Trigger. After the Mark II came the TF, and some of these were screwed out to a full 1½ liters—sturdy but slow. Thorough sports cars, they were not designed to be winners against anything but each other.

After the TF came the MG A, in appearance a small copy of an XK120 Jag, and these were faster, but the competition by then was also much faster. After the plain MG A came, of all things, the TC again, only in this case the "TC" stood for "Twin Cam," and the opposition was still much faster in the 1½-liter class. The guy who wrote "too little, too late" must have been on the Board of Directors.

The MG, despite the above, is still one of the nicest-handling cars in the entire world; built to last, these true sports cars have given more people pleasure in owning and driving them than the rest of the pack jammed together. Why they ever allowed themselves to slip so far back in competition is a mystery we believe will never be fully solved—but the guy who owns an MG as a general purpose car will be the owner of a real gem, even though his shelves may remain naked of silverware. At this writing, it seems that the new twin cam engine, in slimmed-down versions, may again make a mark—but I wouldn't bank too heavily on it. Wonder what the next TD will be like?

Porsche

The Porsche is a true connoisseur's sports car, and appreciated only by true connoisseurs. The reason only connoisseurs appreciate it is because, by the wildest stretching of the imagination, it doesn't look like the price tag it carries. Since the Porsche made its first appearance on these shores back in 1952, it has won hundreds of races, and enginewise has proven just about as reliable as heat in summer, cold in winter. It isn't a docile car, and seems to have a facility for rolling over with the greatest of ease when pressed too hard by unskilled hands. In one race the writer attended, where the turns were flat and rough, there were eight flip-overs by Porsche cars—which is hardly the best way to finish. The tendency to flip was caused at least partly by Porsche's split rear axle, which did odd things when bumps occurred and both rear wheels left the pavement. On the return trip to earth, the rear wheels veed, and *away you go*, rolling to left or right, depending on which wheel hit the earth first. Drivers have been killed in these cars, and they are definitely nothing for an untalented leadfoot to fool with. They are great machines, in the hands of great drivers, but not for the neophyte to do his first racing in.

Jaguar

Bill Lyons' Jaguars come in as many models and colors as Greek confetti and have always been one of the best dollar-for-dollar buys offered in the entire automobile world. In many cases these cars, unlike the Porsche, look as though they cost more than they do. Quality is the finest the price tag can possibly allow, and whether you buy a small convertible coupe, a medium or large size saloon or an out-and-out competition rig, there is nothing better in the world for sale at the price. Competition Jags sell for considerably less than many makes that have proven inferior to them on the race courses of the world. Jaguars have used the world's hardest race courses as their proving grounds, and their record at LeMans is better than any other make ever, though they were quite often the least expensive car in their days in the ratrace. At this writing, competition Jaguars hold the European sedan record—oh hell, when you talk about competition you can get into a lather about everything from Mercedes to Ferraris, but the Jaguar reliability factor is one of the greatest testimonials that you can buy a fine-handling, winning sports car of quality without owning half the Bank of England.

Aston-Martin

Aston-Martin has never sold on these shores as a mass-produced product, or even in great quantity, but is nevertheless a connoisseur's bucket as sexy-looking as any $18,000 Ferrari, and with a much friendlier price tag. Of all the sports cars selling for under $10,000, the Aston is perhaps the most exclusive prestige sports car you can possibly buy. The coupes, though they can be raced, are rarely seen in competition these days, perhaps because they are just too expensive to bend, or too nice to mess up.

Austin-Healey

Austin-Healey, the big brother of the MG, has, like the Jaguar, a barrel of style, good looks, fair performance; but, again like the Jaguar, it's a lot of sports car for the money. It's thoroughly reliable, easy to service, and an excellent touring sports car for a man, wife, and not-oversized dog. Theoretically a four place car, the specifications of the rear seat require passengers to be considerably limited in size, if any comfort is to be experienced. The typical A-H six might best be explained as a "sports car for the sportsman with only mild competition interest." However, for some time they have dominated the D Production class. It's an excellent buy and a car that you can have a lot of fun in and with. It handles beautifully, has an extremely comfortable ride for a car of this type, and $3,500 will more than cover the transaction.

Mercedes

Since the first car the writer ever rode in (when he was a ripe six weeks old) was a Mercedes, and since my father once owned nine of them, this, to me, has always been *the* automobile among automobiles. Unfortunately, the Mercedes available to the buying public have not been (with the slight exception of the 300SL) winning-type sports cars. Mercedes are built in two sizes: one for the factory teams and one for the peasants who buy them—and nearly all relationship stops there. The 190SL roadster is as pleasant a sports car to drive as anyone could hope for, and with quality literally oozing from its seams. However, it is not over-athletic, and to me the whole line seems extremely over-priced—by about 25% on each model as sold in this country. For those wishing to buy a Mercedes abroad, the deal is much more realistic, since the cars somehow seem to this writer to have gotten a real hard mark-up pad once they hit the North American continent. Great cars—great talking pieces—but actually not too exciting from a sports standpoint. The new detachable hardtop 300SL is a two-seater with enough Teutonic magnetism to curl the mustache on an old-time Newport dowager.

Alfa Romeo

A name as sexy as the Place Pigalle, the Alfa Romeo south and east of the Alps commands the respect the name "Mercedes" does in Germany. Alfa Romeo was the only serious competition Mercedes faced during the years when Hitler was calling the signals by direct wire to the pits. The Alfa Romeo at this writing is offering its nice spider convertible that looks every inch a champion. Its athletic abilities on these shores have failed to raise many eyebrows, however, with the exception of the G Production Class, which the Giulietta Spider has dominated for some time. These are great cars as saloon talking pieces—easy to get serviced in the metropolitan areas, and with a touch of exclusiveness that you won't find with more commonplace offerings.

Arnolt-Bristol

The Arnolt-Bristol, a combination Anglo-American-Italian bucket manufactured in England for S. H. Arnolt of Chicago, gets its body from Italy and its good wishes from "Wacky" Arnolt, who pays the bills. This just-under-two-liter car is a real racing connoisseur's rig. Moderately expensive, it has the exclusive touch desired by many, and in its class, E Production, has copped many a piece of silverware. This is a deluxe piece of sporting equipment available on order in several models.

Ferrari

When you talk about Ferrari, if your grandfather happened to be a gondola jockey, a slight bend of the knee and a bow towards Modena is in order. Ferraris come in more sizes and combinations than dice in a Nevada bounce house, and all have one thing in common —expense. The Ferrari is top-drawer money stuff, and, whether the buyer is contemplating winning strictly Grand Prix, unlimited sports car, or class sports car events, the only way he can do better than entering with a Ferrari is to shoot all the officials and give it a go on a scooter. Enzo Ferrari may or may not build a car for you, depending on how he feels on the day he gets the order. Ferraris have won everything from LeMans to the Grand Prix at Daytona Beach, and have made more drivers famous in the last ten years than Judge Murtagh of New York's Traffic Courts. They don't always win, but everytime Ferraris are entered in a race they are the cars to beat, and the jockeys who drive them, from Phil Hill and Carrol Shelby to just about all the top Latin wheel twirlers, would form a blue ribbon crop of driving celebrities. If you know about Ferraris and how to drive them, you won't need any tips from me. If you're not familiar with Ferraris, then *don't*—it's no car to start with.

Triumph

The Triumph, a Class E roadster selling for just over $2,600 is, from a dollar-for-dollar standpoint, one of the greatest sports car buys available. With 105-plus mph top speed, turned out by a beautiful four-cylinder overhead-valve engine as reliable as whiskers on a coal miner, there just isn't anything better at the price. Top roadability, agility, and excellent disc brakes in the front make this a great beginner's (or old-timer's) sports car. One drawback, to the writer, is its looks. Not too much imagination or styling is reflected in this slab-sided gold nugget—but then, you can't have everything at a price, and it *will* outrun sports cars selling for a great deal more money. A top buy in any league.

There are literally ten sports cars available for every stock American model made. Some of the better-known would include the American Corvette, which is an excellent big-company attempt at a sideline article; the great BMW, one of Germany's top production automobiles, with a V8 engine; the Elva; the Lotus; the Fraser-Nash; the Gordini from France; the Gregoire; the Lancia from Italy; the Maserati; the Facel-Vega rally car, made in France but powered by a big Chrysler engine; the DKW of West Germany; the Abarth and the Morgan. In fact, just about every sports car fan in Europe with a workable screwdriver, hammer and wrench, plus a tin-pile, has at one time or another built a sports car. We won't attempt to cover all of them, since the better ones are continually undergoing changes. Your best bet for keeping up with new models and changes is any one of several foreign magazines such as *Autocar* or *Motor*. The best American offering is *Road & Track*, which has become the bible of the sports car fraternity.

4

Rally Cars

RALLY CARS COME IN JUST ABOUT AS MANY SHAPES and sizes as you can dream up. In fact, in most cases, no limitations exist. In some big-time events, rallies may be restricted to closed saloons (known over here as sedans), but in recent times, just about every rally has been an open event where cars ranging from station wagons to roadsters are eligible. However, for many years, the sedan-type car was considered the only true rally car.

Rally cars in this country are most commonly thought of as small economical sedans like the Saab, Volkswagen, Hillman, Austin and others of this type. These smaller offerings, comparatively inexpensive, are at an advantage in some rallies because their manageable size makes them quick to maneuver over third-rate roads and twisty trails. Add to this the fact that in most cases they have better traction than their larger counterparts, and the reason for selecting them is tough to argue with. For example, take a course where there is a strong possibility of getting off the road and into a snowbank—or even miring down in mud. It is a lot easier to extract one of these featherweights than to yank out an Imperial. Also with the lighter car, you're not quite so apt to go as far into a snowbank or into the mud.

Cars of this type, which also includes the Morris Minor, DKW, Simca, Vauxhall and Opel, have one *dis*-advantage in a major rally, and that may come when, due to such unforeseen circumstances as bad navigation, a roadblock, or a short journey into a snowbank, the driver and navigator find they have considerable time to make up in order to stay in the competition at all. Let's take an imaginary oversimplified case. On the leg between Petunia and Asparagus (some 50 miles) you're supposed to average 40 mph on the nose. However, during the night it snowed heavily, and though you are the 20th car off the line, when you reach the mountain peak, 20 miles from the start, you find several cars off the road and your path through is entirely blocked. Or let's be sporting and assume you go off the road, too. Extracting the car or getting through the roadblock consumes, let's say, 20 minutes. Your time allotted for the whole leg (and in this case we are ruling out secret checkpoints) is one hour and fifteen minutes. Your car was stopped by the blockade or by going off the road at the 20-mile point, and you had been averaging exactly 40 mph up until then. You had already consumed 30 minutes. Add to this a 20-minute delay, and you suddenly find you still have 30 miles to go and only 25 minutes to do them in. In other words, to hit your checkpoint on the nose you must average 72 mph the rest of the distance. Fortunately, you are doing this in a country where there are no speed limits, and there are no towns between you and your destination, but there are a number of hard bends and curves, and one or two up-and-down grades, which mean much of the time during the next 25 minutes you'll have to be running 80 mph or better to average 72 mph.

The point of this whole thing was to show you that when unforseen things do crop up (as they usually do in the well-known annual events), the smaller-powered, lower-speed cars with time to make up will be at a decided disadvantage, because in our imaginary case such cars as the VW, Saab and Dauphine just can't go 80 mph, (unless you own a Gran Turismo Saab). This goes for most of the other low-powered jobs too. In the case mentioned, the Swedish Volvo, with a top between 95 and 100 mph, would be just what the doctor ordered—or even a Rambler American, with a top speed of 85 mph, might be able to squeeze in, as would a 3.4 Jag and other more powerful machines.

Rallies have been won by Dauphines and Imperials, but this doesn't necessarily mean that either is the ideal rally car. Conditions at the casual, Sunday-afternoon-type rally, except for traffic, rarely make it necessary to own a semi-high-speed car. For the serious rally man, a little extra speed reserve is a handy package to have in your bag of tricks.

Volkswagen

Undoubtedly, the most popular rally-type car is the German Volkswagen. With a top speed of just over 70 mph, it handles like a feather, will go practically anywhere a Jeep will in dry terrain and is about as indestructable as sex. VWs have won the toughest rally of all, the Redex round-Australia grind, a win that used to be reserved for modified Fords. The VW gets better than 35 miles to a gallon of gas, can cruise from New York to

Chicago on the turnpikes at 65 mph plus, and has become the small car standard of the world. The VW is capable of winning any of the world's rallies, but, as pointed out, if it should get far behind at one point in a particularly fast rally, it may not be able to make up enough time, and in steep mountainous country with switchbacks that slow your progress to a walk at times, its small, air-cooled engine may lose considerable time off a high speed average. However, because of its rear-engine design it is far better balanced to attack snow and ice than any American car, and most other imports that aren't also rear-engine drive. One bad fault the VW has as a rally car is that the odometer is not divided into tenths. This creates an impossible situation even for the Saturday-afternoon rallyist. Replacement heads can be had, though, with a trip meter measuring in tenths for around 25 or more dollars—and this expenditure is a must. In fact, quite a few of the small rally-type cars are delivered with the VW-type tenth-less odometer. This should bc checked before purchase, since, without the correct odometer, you might just as well compete on a tricycle.

Renault Dauphine

This little French counterpart of the VW won the 1958 Monte Carlo Rally. It is a four-door sedan with a liquid-cooled engine located in the rear. Its brake horsepower is rated at 30 and top speed is just about 70 mph. These are fine little inexpensive cars, and good for a rally —but don't get far behind time.

Saab

Here is a two-cycle, three-cylinder-engined car without a crankcase. Oil is added directly to the gas—similar to most outboard marine engines. It has front wheel drive, fabulous roadability, and one of the greatest rally records of any car being made today. In out-and-out races it has proven the fastest of the under-$2,000 import cult, and with its many unusual features, is a true connoisseur's car. A Gran Turismo model of this car should prove an ideal rally rig, though the price is a third more. It comes equipped with instruments and a high performance engine for immediate rally competition. The car is made in Sweden and put together like a fine watch, but extreme care should be used during the break-in period, partially because of its off-beat lubrication system.

Volvo

This Swedish gem, somewhat resembling a 1946 Ford, is the king of the small car field selling for less than $2500. In showroom tune, it'll top 95 mph and will do 100 mph after a thorough break-in and a good tune up. It is now sold with a magnificent four-speed gearbox, and one of the finest engines being built in the world today. It displaces just over a liter and half.

In Europe two other Volvo models are available that make the American import look rather dowdy. These are the Amazon and a sports convertible, both of which are pure glamor, but to this writing only a few have drifted into America, after having been bought in Europe by servicemen. If Volvo sales should ever get rough in this country the glamor models will undoubtedly be brought over, but at this writing the Volvo, since it's being sold today with a price tag of roughly $2,300, is one of the greatest buys in the world, and I doubt if you could find a better all-around rally car at any price.

Simca

The Simca sedan and convertible now being imported are top-grade French products, and the American

Chrysler Corporation has bought an important interest in them. The Simca comes in a number of models from the Aronde and Montlery to a pretty sexy convertible, the Oceane. They range in speed depending on model from 85 to 90 mph, and must be considered a good rally prospect.

German Ford Taunus

This is a beautifully-built small vehicle with better-than-average small-car performance, but, in the jobs this writer tested, was low in the traction department, and therefore hardly a candidate for snow-and-ice work.

Morris Minor

Another of the more popular imports, this small job, with its top speed of about 70 mph, is perhaps one of the finest-handling cars in the entire world. It has excellent clearance and reliability, but in a snow-and-ice rally it is advised that weight be carried in the trunk, because in the traction department it is no match for such cars as the VW. In test cars that failed to take an icy hill the addition of one passenger in the rear seat would make it go up and over like a puff of smoke. A hundred pound bag of sand in the trunk would have the same effect.

Rambler American

This popular Kenosha, Wisconsin entry is price-wise and quality-wise a match for any import selling for less than $2,000. However, for hard rallies it does not have the stability or roadability of cars like the Saab or Volvo, and is a little tail-light for snow work. It does have, however, an economical six cylinder L-head engine that gives the car a top speed of 85 mph. A few inexpensive alterations like firmer shocks and a little trunk weight could make this Rambler an important rally entry.

This is only a smattering of the available cars; there are dozens more that might fit your rally bill to a T, such as the DKW, or even the small Goggomobil which has won rallies. Then there's the German Goliath, Hillman, Vauxhall and Opel, Fiat, English Ford Zephyr, Consul, Alfa-Romeo—there are dozens.

In buying a car for rally work, your pocketbook may possibly be a guiding factor. Tossing this essential to the winds, let's consider what an ideal rally car might be. Small enough for easy maneuvering and extracting from ditches, it must have quick steering, roadability and traction. It should also be extremely comfortable, because discomfort on a rally is very tiring, and this is when goofs start showing up and driving errors occur. Take the Gran Turismo Saab—this might be an ideal standard to set, because it's capable of winning any rally in the world, under the right conditions. The only drawback is that in climbing icy slopes it's front wheel drive doesn't seem to be able to match the push of the rear-wheel-drive cars, but the Saab did take one great snow rally by backing up over an icy pass.

A Volkswagen with correct odometer and rally instruments and a Porsche engine for more speed and power would prove a pretty hard combination to beat. This rig, however, might cross you up in coming down icy slopes, especially if you are not used to counter-correcting skids and slides by using just the opposite methods brought to play with front-engined cars. Often, with a rear engined car that gets into trouble on ice or a bad bend, the best correction is to hit the brakes or turn with the slide and get another grip. The methods for correcting a more conventional car are discussed fully in our chapter on driving.

The ideal way to win rallies is to own several cars to match various climates, courses and speeds. In many rallies, sports cars such as the Triumph are not only allowed, but used. Sports cars naturally have many more athletic properties than even the finest rally sedans, but we are now talking about a rally stable owned by a guy with a barge full of gold bullion and a valid map to where a lot more is buried. This guy might very well have a Triumph, Jag or Porsche for his weekend rally runs. He could even get real extreme and reach way into the bag and come up with a field-trial-winning Dellow for climbing muddy or icy slopes, as the Dellow would almost go up the wall to the 56th floor of the Chrysler building. He might also pick a car such as the 3.4 Jag for more blustery weather, or he might buy an Aston-Martin or even a Ferrari coupe.

But before I get carried away too far, let's get back to the typical character who wants a small car as his one-and-only or second car for his wife when he's not borrowing it for some national rally. He wants to do this without mortgaging the family homestead and grandpa's beard. If he wants to spend less than $2,000, the Saab with its superior speed might be a wise choice; it has won more rallies than Stassen got votes in the Pennsylvania primary. Bearing this in mind, he still wouldn't go very far wrong with a VW and a few added instruments and alterations. If he can stretch just above $2,000, the Volvo would be an outstanding choice. Beyond this, there's nothing to match the Volvo in performance until you reach the 3.4 Jag.

Under some circumstances, American cars like the Chrysler 300, and even the rally-winning Imperial, can be used successfully, but as an all-around rally car it would hardly be my choice, and I own an Imperial for general travel use. All American cars with sloppy suspension and poor balance would be at a decided disadvantage, with the exception of the Rambler American reworked with tough shocks, and even at that the Volvo would kill it. As Steve Brodie once said, "We have 'em for two bucks, five bucks, and ten bucks—the ten dollar ones are cleaner."

5

High-Performance American Cars

THOUGH IT MAY RUFFLE UP THE FUZZ ON MANY a tweed cap, there have been some great American high-performance cars built in recent years. Oddly enough, between the publishing of *The Modern Sports Car* in 1954 and the present quite a cycle took place in the Michigan stamping houses.

In 1955, a team of Chrysler cars, backed by Carl Kiekhaefer, an outboard motor manufacturer, started blanketing nearly all the winning positions in major stock-car races. With a slight nod to a "For-God's-Sake-Get-Going" command from the top level in Ford and General Motors, American manufacturers soon found themselves up to their armpits in competition. Millions of dollars were poured into the effort of trying to win competitions that ranged all the way from the Pike's Peak Climb and the Darlington "500" to winning the speed trials at Daytona Beach. At Daytona one winter, the budget for one major camp passed the million dollar mark. When successful runs had been made, or races won, this news was blasted to the entire world through every known advertising media. Ed Sullivan on Sunday nights would give the results of Mercury's or Lincoln's accomplishments for that day (if they'd won) and Ford, Chevrolet, Pontiac, and the rest would work into the last-second copy information pertaining to their successes, when they had them. The competition even went to the point where, when Chevy was winning everything in its class and bragging in huge ads that they were "The Hot One", along came Ford, and as they started to nip Chevy occasionally, they referred to themselves as "The Car that Cooled the Hot One." Actually, it was all a lot of fun, and nothing more serious than getting fired faced a losing group of engineers.

Before the Edict of 1957

The big swirl in factory-backed competition lasted only a short time, ending on June 6th, 1957, when the Automobile Manufacturers Association as a group voted to ban all factory participation in any form of competition. To this mandate were added a lot of side clauses, including one to the effect that regardless of who backed the car that won any competition, no mention of it would be made in any form of advertising, promotion or press release. On that day in June the factories washed their hands clean of racing and competition forever.

This was a black day for the American automobile-buying public. In less than three years, American cars had advanced more than they had in the preceding quarter of a century. The reason was simple. The manufacturers just couldn't stand seeing their own team cars snapping wheels on turns, collapsing with cracked frames, running out of brakes, or rolling over due to mushiness. When these things happened, as many as 100,000 people witnessed the spectacle, and the results spread like wildfire to anyone who might contemplate buying the failing make of car.

At one big race, eleven different cars of one make snapped right front wheels in the same mildly hard turn. Soon afterward, this particular brand of car gained the best wheel-staying-on batting average of any make on the tracks. Even though that was some time ago, the writer still receives mail telling him about the dangerous wheels on such-and-such a car, citing the day it dropped the eleven right front wheels. Another weakness brought to light by racing and later corrected was spindles snapping with all the regularity of sundown.

American cars became safer and better than ever before due to these racing efforts. When drivers started being killed in rollovers and light crashes because doors popped open, spewing them onto the tracks, the manufacturers went into a great campaign to improve their doorlocks. Today's doorlocks are better, but far from perfect—and in the big-time circuits such as NASCAR, doors must still be *bolted closed and strapped* before a car is allowed to race. Though the front wheel and axle assemblies were improved to a point where they were safer than ever before, NASCAR encouraged still further beefing up of these units because stock front ends were still collapsing.

The 1957 American automobiles (those that were racing) were perhaps the finest-performing, safest automobiles ever built in this country. With the edict of June '57, this writer predicted that you could look for a backward step in a year or two, and that step came in the 1959 models of many cars. Suspension began softening up again, and even over-the-ground performance had slipped quite a few notches, except in one camp (that was founded by Walter P. Chrysler).

In 1959 all Chrysler cars still had torsion bar suspension which may have resulted from their racing experience. In 1959 these cars were head-and-shoulders over any other American make not only from the standpoint of safety, but of roadability, comfort, and ease of handling. The other camps, claiming that research had shown that America really wanted a soft, charlotte-russe ride, went into types of suspension that employed everything from nightmarish air bags to soft-acting coils. Safer firmness and stability were over the hill.

The Aftermath

We still have, at this writing, a number of holdovers from racing. Oddly enough, from a sporting standpoint, the edict to abandon competition caught some manufacturers just on the brink of greatness, but not quite over. Not all company or division heads liked this non-competition move, and among them is rumored to be Ed Cole, headman at Chevy, who had developed the 1956 Chevrolet into a car that could break under nine seconds for 0-60 mph, and crack over 130 mph with ease, when properly tuned.

Cole's Corvette was close to becoming one of the world's great competition sports cars when the boom was dropped (and the same may be said about Ford, but not to such a degree). Factory-owned Ford Thunderbirds and Chevy Corvettes registered better than 150 mph at the Daytona Beach Speed Trials before the axe fell. The next year, the fastest four-place Thunderbird averaged 107, and the fastest Corvette 135 mph.

Pontiac, headed by Semon E. "Bunky" Knudsen, had taken over from Chevrolet the title of General Motor's hottest offering back in '57, when it won not only the speed trials at Daytona Beach, but the feature race as well. In 1958, this great Pontiac engine won the flying mile championship with one run of 144 mph. Here, a two-door Pontiac sedan went 9 mph faster than the fastest Corvette, and 37 mph faster than the then-new four-place Thunderbird.

All was not completely lost, however. Lance Reventlow took stock Corvette engines and worked them into his Scarab, the first American sports car sensation since Briggs Cunningham with his Cunningham cars started dominating the American sports car scene back in 1951.

There are good American cars and there are poor American cars, but some of the better high-performance cars are phenomenally good. Nothing made in Europe in the sedan or saloon class can stay with our hotter offerings. Cars like the Chrysler 300 can outrun any sedan in the world on any sports car course. The big Chrysler 300 can top 140 mph, and, due to its excellent suspension, can drill through a corner or bend with any of the touring-type sports cars. The American cars don't have the brakes of the top sports cars, but they really have no need for them in everyday use.

On the other hand, let's not lose sight of the fact that back in '58 an American sedan went around the Bridgehampton race course for 100 miles only one mph slower than the winning Lister-Jaguar did just the month before. When American stock cars are put in the hands of such men as Smokey Yunick, Red Vogt, Bill Stroppe and a host of others, with a little working here and a twist there, which includes beefing up the suspension in some cases, they'll give all but the top racing sports cars a hard run in any terrain—and they do it carrying fantastic weight, comparatively, and with a body shape hardly calculated for Grand Prix work.

Detroit Today

Because the writer was the first ever to criticize American cars in print, the first to call them monsters, "Detroit Iron," and refer to "Jello Suspension," in fact, the first writer ever to hint that Detroit company heads were not automatically qualified for election to the College of Cardinals, and the first ever to call them frauds, mountebanks and liars, I believe it should be my province to point out when some of them have made real advancements. Quality and quality control in Michigan are still horrible things to behold, and bodywork may resemble the product of a Japanese toy factory. Tie this up with the ludicrous advertising that often accompanies these balloons and you'll soon see that craftsmanship left the United States with the *Monitor* and the *Merrimac*, but in its place came some pretty clever engineering gimmicks—some good, some horrible. The typical American car is a pretty tawdry industrial product, but it definitely has something worthwhile to offer—and even the guys with two points on their heads would have a hard time arguing against that.

Let's get the picture square in our minds first. Very few American cars attempt to sell quality—it's non-existent when compared with cars such as the Rolls, Bentley or top-grade Mercedes. Where these imports top us most is in body work and luxurious appointments. Our synthetics and snap-on panels are no match for the import's quality, but if you look way down deep there is still a heart of pure gold to find—and it's usually found in the engine and chassis. Take any Ford, Plymouth, or Chevrolet, drive it intelligently, don't hit anything harder than a breadbox and have it serviced regularly. You'll breeze through the first hundred thousand miles without any more trouble than replacing the spark plugs, ignition points, brakes, tires, and battery. Your engine will still be sound and ready to go for another hundred thousand with reasonable care and a few minor overhauls—a valve job and possibly rings. True, the seats may be sat-out, the body shabby, the rugs shot, and the hardware sketchy in operation, *but they'll keep going.*

Now, on the typical expensive import, to go 100,000 miles without a major overhaul would be like walking into Grant's Tomb and finding the old gentleman still breathing. These are facts, not fancy, as any honest import dealer will tell you. Bear in mind also that, in most cases, even our most expensive cars cost less than half the price of the good imports, and you have quite a case. In 1953, I had a Mexican Road Race Lincoln built up for me. This was one of the hot ones screwed together right, and with genuine fine leather upholstery. I sold the car when it had 48,000 miles on it. The last time I saw it was in early '59. It had passed 250,000 miles, and had had new valves at 200,000, a ring job at the same time (no reboring), the upholstery still looked good, and the original paint was in fine shape. As far as I know, this car is still going, being used every day. Though this was a special car, it sold for only $6,000 back in '53. Hardly a junkpile—and because of its then-called "export suspension" (locally called "competition suspension") it could drill through a corner like a Scotch-taped eel.

There are a number of high-performance cars built in America that are worthy vehicles in anyone's league, and if you've never been to a big-time late-model stock car race on a big course circuit, then go—and get bug-eyed. The drivers of these cars have fantastic ability, which many of them acquired originally as ridge runners on the moonshine circuit. When it comes to cornering and powerslides, some of these boys on the stock car circuit couldn't even borrow a comma from Tazio Nuvolari's book. I realize this will sound like heresy in some Tattersall-vest sets, but the idea of this book is to give a true picture of what is going on in the automotive world today.

I'll always remember the time when Phil Walters was America's outstanding sports car driver and I was at the same table with him at the annual dinner of the Sports Car Club of America. Someone asked him, "If money was no object, what kind of a car would you want for yourself?" Without hesitation, he answered, "A nice big American car with automatic transmission and air conditioning." The asker all but fainted—he was one of the types of little boys who likes to play store on rainy days.

6

Antique Cars

NOBLE STEEDS OF THE PAST HAVE BECOME A nationwide hobby in the past few years. All likely hiding places, such as barns on estates, warehouses, and automobile graveyards have, by this time, been pretty thoroughly combed by collectors and connoisseurs for rare old pieces of transportation to restore and bring back to life. Men like Henry Austin Clark (known to the warden as "Austy"), James "The Tenor" Melton and numerous others have compiled large collections of old cars for the public to view at very nominal fees—(fees which just about pay for maintenance). Clark's Museum in Southampton, Long Island and Melton's in Hypoluxo, Florida, are two of the very best, but there are many others and in nearly every state. The Henry Ford Museum in Dearborn, Michigan contains some pieces of real interest to the antique car fan. The Antique Automobile Club of America and the Horseless

Carriage Club are two major associations that have gone deeply into cars of the past, and deserve recognition for the good work they've done as the guardians of these historic milestones.

Several times we've sent teams of antique cars abroad to compete with English teams, and these cars were actually raced in competition against each other. Antique car racing is very rare in the East, except for mild gymkhana-type events, but at one Wichita, Kansas, rally the writer attended, where dozens of the finest restored antiques he had ever seen were gathered, these fine old masterpieces were not only raced, but I mean *really* raced, around a small oval track at Joyland Park in Wichita. In addition they had *drag* races with as many as a dozen cars at a time racing abreast over a tenth-of-a-mile course—and all this with the temperature tickling 100 degrees Fahrenheit.

The writer raced a tiller-steered Locomobile steam car owned by Herb Ottaway which had been restored to all the lustre of a freshly-polished Sultan's jewel. When I opened the throttle, this nearly-60-year-old wonder shot away like an arrow released from a hundred-pound bow. If you've never tried broadsliding around a turn nearly six feet off the ground with tiller steering, then you just haven't lived. For thrills, this packs more jollies than getting an electric massage at Sing Sing. In the first big race, my assistant, Jim McMichael, was standing on the inside of one corner where he deemed beforehand it would be safe to take photographs. What he didn't know (and neither did I) was that these Kansas boys don't fool around! Six abreast, cars ranging from a 1907 Maxwell to 1909 Reo tried to fit in a slot only three cars wide. Two sailed off the track, and one bore right down on McMichael, who jumped for safety, which he made by the skin of his head, saying, "To hell with the pictures." As Jim, who has taken hundreds of pictures of sports car races and high performance tests, said later, "This was the closest call I ever had. Imagine what a disgrace it would have been to be killed by a Jack Benny 1907 Maxwell!"

Naturally, if the boys keep playing this way, there won't be many antiques left when the relatives drop in from the moon for a visit fifty years from now, but what's even more important, the guys who restored them are having fun with them, and though there was some minor damage to some of these Tiffany-like pieces, you can take it from me, antique-car racing, as they do it in Wichita, is not for chickens. As I saw it in Kansas, it was just as much a competitive sport as any Grand Prix I've ever seen—the only difference was the mounts were just a little older.

7

Buying a Used Sports Car

BUYING A SECOND-HAND SPORTS CAR CAN EASILY be compared to a guy looking forward to a long, happy married life with a gal who's already been married eight times. Unless you know the *real, complete* history of a second-hand sports car from the day it left the factory, you may find yourself with a lemon slightly larger than the state of Rhode Island.

That old American used-car salesman's dodge that "This car belonged to an old maid school teacher [or a sickly old minister] who had to dispose of it because of her arthritis," just ain't so. The chances are 99 in 100 that the second-hand sports car you are considering was formerly owned by a red-blooded demon who spent hours over-revving the engine, crashing the gears, and bending it around hairpin turns. There are exceptions to this, but I believe they are as rare as finding a herd of elephants in the Maine woods.

Before getting too interested in buying a second-hand sports car, here are a couple of suggestions that may help. If the price is extremely low, you may be getting a real bargain or a super lemon; do your best to find out which, as there *are* some real sports car bargains.

Every second-hand sports car should be approached with all the gingerness of disarming an unexploded land mine. As a general rule, if it is at all possible financially, *avoid* buying someone else's castoff toy. The original owner might have never raced the car, or clashed the gears, but he may have given in to that almost-uncontrollable urge of trying to see how fast it would go in the first 200 miles.

The average sports car engine calls for a lot more careful breaking in than does a standard Detroit product. In the first place, much lighter and quicker-expanding metals are used, and clearance tolerances are a lot finer than called for in Michigan. If the engine has been forced after clearances have been reduced to zero through expansion, a number of unpleasant things may result. Pistons may be collapsed or re-shaped. Valves may be warped or bent. Bearings may be scarred, or entire engine blocks or heads may be distorted permanently.

The average new sports car engine should be run for short periods only, and with an eagle-eye peeled at all times for the slightest signs of overheating or resistance. If these signs appear, the engine should be shut off immediately, even though you may be half way to the grave yard in your grandmother's funeral procession. We'll tell you more about breaking in later, but we'll just mention this now, so that you can fairly ask yourself what the chances are that the car you are contemplating was broken in this way.

By another token, just to keep the records mixed up,

there are a number of buyers who specialize (successfully) in purchasing cars that have already proven themselves in races. Such fanciers are usually fully equipped with money and technical knowledge to cope with any unpleasantness that might crop up.

Sports cars, like anything else produced, have their hot numbers and slow numbers. For example, the chances are that in any hundred sports cars, as they arrive on the dock, one will be exceptionally fast and several will be slower than average.

What causes this difference may vary from group to group, but the exceptional cars, once proven, always find a ready market. Once in a blue moon a real used-stock bomb turns up, and this car is worth more to the competition buyer than he would have to pay for a brand-new one of the same make and model. For the average sports car purchaser, these "drops from heaven" rarely appear. Buying a second-hand sports car off a dealer's lot can easily turn into a real "sporty" adventure.

In cars such as the MG or Jag, repairs can be cheap compared to those made on the costlier, rarer products. A used Ferrari that has been raced in everything but the Kentucky Derby could easily cost a fortune before it would run from your house to the drugstore. A little repair bill of over a thousand dollars on a Ferrari might be the bargain of the year. Unless a great Ferrari specialist gave the car an O.K., I wouldn't buy a used Ferrari if Nelson Rockefeller promised to act as a hood ornament.

Before investing your good dollars in a used sports car, there are precautions that can be taken to keep you from becoming Mr. Chump of the Year. If the car is offered for sale and guaranteed by a firm such as J. S. Inskip in New York, you have very little to worry about. Inskip stands behind its guarantees 100 per cent, and

Ferrari coupe ready to race at Sebring—an outstanding specimen of today's high-powered competition machine.

Hardly the car for a family outing, this competition Maserati in tune for Sebring.

Modern road racing demands the skill of the experienced pro or semi-pro, in the pit and in the cockpit.

At Wichita, Kansas, the author takes over the glamor queen of today—a brand-new 1959 Silver Cloud Rolls-Royce belonging to George Sharpe—for a test run on the fairgrounds.

Throwing the Rolls into a full broadslide shows the remarkable handling qualities these royal pieces are seldom called upon to display.

A connoisseur of the first order: Briggs S. Cunningham, 1958 skipper of the America's Cup Defender Columbia *and the man who has done the most for sports car racing in this country, shown here with the author at a race.*

Briggs Cunningham (right) with Alfred Momo, another man who has helped build sports car racing in America, in Briggs's Lister-Jaguar before the start of a race.

The author's assistant, Jim McMichael, demonstrates the value of the sliding sun roof when a tall man takes to a Porsche.

Another connoisseur, Paul Whiteman, "The Jazz King," shown with his Super Porsche and the author.

Mixed bag of small production gems under way in Florida race.

Currently Technical Director of the American Jaguar Team, here Alfred Momo backs a Lister-Jaguar into its slot at Sebring.

MGA straightening out after extra-hard broadslide which moved several hundred pounds of real estate.

Competition Aston-Martin in race trim.

Object of no little curiosity: the Mercedes air brake at LeMans.

Austin-Healey racing coupe ready to do its stuff.

It's evident that anyone who takes the wheel inside this competition Ferrari cockpit means business. The instruments from left to right are: oil temperature gauge, oil pressure gauge, tachometer, fuel indicator, and speedometer.

Triumph team before the start of the Sebring 12-Hours. These inexpensive two-seaters with their 100-MPH-plus speed are among the most popular of all small sports cars available today.

Elva (compounded from the French ella va*: she goes), small English production sports car, at Sebring.*

Deutsch-Bonnet, small rally car popular in Europe.

Fiat-Albarth coupe at Sebring.

Dealer Jim Mezey demonstrates good points of the Saab to the author.

Another small import, the Taunus, made in Germany for Ford Motor Company.

English-made, American-owned Vauxhall, parked in front of the author's boat.

America's answer to the small imported rally car, the Rambler American, shown with the author and his field trial champion, Boji Boy, on Daytona Beach.

the firm has never been known to misrepresent any car it has ever sold.

There are some dealers, however, in the hinterlands (*and* New York) who could easily qualify for Jack-the-Ripper scholarships in any big racketeer's domain. If the car you are contemplating belongs to an individual seller, it would be wise to have a sports car mechanical expert check it over for signs of abuse and wear.

To sum up this used sports car situation, there are good used sports cars available, but, as a general rule, I would just as soon buy a used snake.

8

Breaking in Your Sports Car

UNFORTUNATELY, MANY GOOD CARS ARE FAIRLY worn out before they've traveled 1,000 miles. Many dealers and salesmen are directly guilty for not taking the first-time sports car buyer aside and explaining the facts of life.

In America 95 per cent of sports car buyers have previously driven only Detroit products, many of which are designed with a driver-stupidity factor built in. Automatic chokes and many similar gadgets are mute testimony to this.

The majority of American cars are built with wider tolerances and with metals that can stand a lot more initial abuse than a highly-tuned, precision-fitted sports car. With a number of our automobiles it is quite possible to abuse them severely from the first mile and not have any noticeable consequences pop up for the next 20,000 miles or so—though they will crop up later.

In the typical sports car engine, much finer and lighter metals, designed for performance, are used. These are fitted with minimum tolerance. The former Detroit owner, treating his new sports car in a Detroit break-in manner, may very well have his engine seize up or even have a wheel bearing freeze, if he isn't lucky.

Somewhere there is a parallel between most Detroit cars and sports cars and a cheap production watch versus a 23-jewel masterpiece. Many's the two-dollar watch that has withstood dozens of falls and still kept going, but rare is the expensive, jeweled timepiece able to survive without injury a drop from the bureau to the floor. Just as a box brownie will still take pictures after being used as a football, the expensive camera is quick to fail if mistreated.

What Happens in the Engine

Try putting yourself in the engine's place (and, believe me, some engines are almost human). Here is roughly what goes on.

Let's assume that you've been lucky enough to buy a sports car that has not been operated as a demonstrator with the speedometer disconnected—regrettably, a common practice. Each moving part, from the main bearings to the camshaft and pistons, was set up at the factory with as close-to-zero tolerances as the manufacturer dared. Some engines have been run-in at the factory, but not all, and few of them to the real hot stage.

Suppose your pride and joy has fewer miles on it than a day-old kitten. You turn the switch, fire it up, and *away* you go. As the engine runs, heat develops, causing expansion. Forced lubrication helps to eliminate friction, but in spite of this there will be considerable wear. Actually, even a well-broken-in engine will get more wear in the first 1,000 miles than it will experience in the next 25,000.

Even the finest-made bearing, crankshaft, camshaft or piston is bound to have a number of microscopic "high" spots. In the case of a bearing (or a piston ring), as this high spot expands the tolerance gets less and less until it's reduced to zero. Then, one of two things must happen. Either the high spot is worn down and off, or it is gouged out. *Something* must give—if it doesn't, the engine will freeze and stop. Naturally, the longer and harder the new engine is run, the more heat is caused by this metal-to-metal rubbing. It won't take the smartest boy in the local beefsteak club to realize that the easier and softer the break-in period, the better the normal break-in wear.

It has always been my practice with new sports car engines never to drive them longer than an hour at a time during the first two or three hundred miles, and also to stop them *immediately* for a cooling-down session if there is any visible sign (or smell) of heat.

Unfortunately, few cars have oil temperature gauges, but if they all did, the crankcase temperature of a new engine would cause a lot of anxiety and result in more care. Quite often, water temperature gauges do not truly reflect extreme heat in the engine's gizzard for some time, and then this water temperature may skyrocket in a matter of a quarter-mile. By this time you might have done some quite serious damage.

Actually, your oil pressure gauge will usually give you a quicker tip-off than the temperature of the coolant because, as expansion takes place inside, it may cause two types of readings on the oil pressure gauge. If the expansion is in an area where it will block oil passage, there may be a sudden unexplained rise in pressure. On the other hand, if the expansion has taken place where there is normal oil resistance, distortion of the expanding part can relieve the pressure in that area and cause a decided drop.

If possible, before even running in your new sports car engine, read the instruction book cover-to-cover. This book will show you the normal oil pressure under average conditions. With this in mind, when the car has reached normal running heat on the water temperature gauge, and as soon as possible, make a note of the oil pressure at a given speed. After this, any notable change one way or the other should immediately make you suspicious.

If there *is* a change, and the heat indicator shows the engine warming up beyond normal, whatever you're doing, *stop!* If you're in the middle of Times Square during the noon-hour rush it's cheaper to get a ticket and pay the fine for obstructing traffic than to continue and ruin your engine.

While still in Times Square, let me point out that to break in any sports car engine in big-city traffic should immediately label you a fugitive from a strait jacket. Traffic driving at a snail's pace with short stops and starts will get your new sports car beauty hotter than a bare-footed Arabian in the middle of an H-bomb blast. If you buy your car in the city, get it on the fast-traffic roads as soon as possible, and either head for the country or Central Park or its equivalent. It'll pay you big dividends in the future if you *stop* every few miles, or not drive more than an hour at a time, and raise the hood and let the engine cool down while you smoke two or three cigarettes, or a pipeful.

By now you may be saying, "This guy McCahill is nuts. I know dozens of people who've bought sports cars in New York or Chicago, and started immediately for California or Florida, non-stop." To these, I would like to say: When I was running two foreign car shops, the fellows who did this paid my rent—and I let 'em have it with both barrels.

Naturally, some sports cars are faster than others, and a break-in speed of 40 mph with an MG could be equivalent of a break-in speed of 70 for the much faster car. So rpm are the pay-off, and almost all real sports cars have tachometers. On a typical sports car it is a wise precaution to keep the rpm under 2,500 for the first 500 miles.

It will also be necessary for your sports car's old age insurance to make at least three oil changes in the first 1,000 miles. I personally recommend the first oil change at 200 miles. In your break-in work, regardless of how gently it's done, all that expanding we've talked about will cause a lot of metal dust and steel shavings (some microscopic in size) to gather in your crankcase. Many sports cars come equipped with oil filters, but not even these can trap all of the metal gook that accumulates during an engine break in. For this reason, I would change the oil again at 500 miles and again at 1,000. After 1,000 miles, if the engine has been carefully used, the major portion of high-spot metal will be worn off or reshaped.

Break-in Oils

Perhaps the question I am most often asked is, "How about break-in oil or special additives?" I have asked nearly all the top factory engineers in this country and abroad about this. The usual answer is, "They don't do any harm." But the experts refuse to discuss various brands, and none I have ever spoken to has *recommended* an additive.

Off the record, however, some of the top men in

this business use additives in their own cars. For example, I know key men in the industry in Europe who privately use an additive in their own competition cars. Over here, I know a number of automotive engineers who, again off the record, use various makes. Some of these additives, unfortunately, cause oil filters to become clogged, and this can be extremely dangerous to the engine.

Personally, I like a good, straight, Pennsylvania oil without a detergent. At times, when I run into a particularly stiff engine, I use a mild, kerosene-base additive, just on the off-chance it might do some good.

Running the Engine at Too-low Speeds

It is rare that piston rings will correctly seat themselves before going at least 2,000 miles. During this period there may be considerable oil burning and the chances of fouling spark plugs are greatly enhanced. For this reason it is just as bad with a new sports car engine to run it at too low speeds—because if you do, nine times out of ten you will be bothered by fouling spark plugs.

It is also bad to run at any constant speed for long periods of time during the break-in period. For example, an absolute steady 60 for three or four hours can cause the engine to get what is known as a "heat set."

Perhaps the best way to run a car during this period, especially when on long stretches such as the New York Thruway, is to alter the speed at intervals so that the fresh engine is subjected to a wide variety of operating heat ranges. It is also good, every once in a while, to wind it up a little for a few seconds—though *never* over 3,000 rpm and *never* when the engine is very hot. This extra opening of the throttle will help sweep out fouling particles that might be gathering inside the combustion chamber.

All my friends who have bought and broken in new sports cars are quick to state that this break-in period is the most agonizing part of owning a sports car. The temptation to find out how quickly your new toy will pass 100 can be sheer torture. The worst situation of all comes when some sneering character in a Detroit frump eyes you, while waiting for a traffic light to change, as if you were a recently-dispossessed tenant from the bottom side of a rock. Only a truly iron will can resist the invitation to try blowing this stroker off when the light goes green.

As tough as these situations are, resist them. After a few thousand miles you will be able to return the glare and then back it up by nailing your Michigan opponent to the ground like a run-over beetle, maybe. Naturally I'm referring to the hotter-performing sports cars. Some of our lesser ones can still be taken by a fast kid on a scooter in a drag race. If you should own one of these under-powered hulks which can only show its sterling qualities when well under way, assume an aloof posture while ignoring the challenges of a hot Pontiac. But back to the break in.

After the Engine Break-in

Ninety-five per cent of automobile owners feel that once their *engine* is broken in, that's all there is to it. *Nothing could be further from the truth.*

All moving chassis parts need careful breaking in. For example, transmission and rear axle gears are more closely fitted than in Detroit products. These expand just like engine parts, and if a high spot is quickly gouged out instead of worn off gently, it is quite possible you'll never know it until the gear lets go, perhaps 15 or 20 thousand miles later. That gouged-out piece of gear may cause a crack that will gradually enlarge until failure results.

Wheel bearings may be set up snug, which will cause expansion at this point. Unless they are worn in to a normal groove before extreme speeds are applied, it is possible to cause an out-of-round bearing race or a complete collapse.

Even springs and shock absorbers should be given a chance to loosen up, and, believe it or not, so should tires. Tires change considerably in weight distribution and contour during the first 500 miles of running. In fact, they change so much it is a real waste of money ever to have a wheel balanced with a brand-new tire. If you do, it will be all out of balance at the end of 500 miles.

This doesn't mean I'm against wheel balancing; it is absolutely essential in any very fast car. But the time to have it done is *not* when you take delivery, but when you come in for your 500 or 1,000 mile service check-up. By this time, the soft spots in your tires have flattened out, and any centralized mass of lumped rubber will have taken a permanent set. Then, and then *only*, is the tire ready for balancing.

Climate and weather conditions affect the correct breaking in of your new sports car. Many sports cars are built with extremely high engine compression ratios, and the higher the compression, the higher the operating temperature. If it were possible I would always buy mine during mid-winter when the temperature is below freezing. At these temperatures, parts expand much more slowly and the same caution won't be called for that confronts the July buyer who takes delivery during a heat wave.

Naturally, this doesn't mean you shouldn't buy a sports car in mid-summer, but it does mean that the mid-summer buyer will have to be more alert for heat than January Jake in Canada. Some really "hot" sports cars with more miles on them than the Toonerville Trolley will overheat on hot summer days without being abused, so it's easy to picture the break-in problem the man who buys this type of car has with a hot-weather delivery.

If you should buy your car in Florida or in July, why not make a game out of it? Get up at four in the morning, while it's still fairly cool, and put 100 or more miles on your car before breakfast. This may sound strange, but this is exactly what a number of my friends have done, and they've enjoyed every minute of it.

Even if you have no intention of driving your new sports car more than 10,000 miles before trading it in on a hotter one, take it easy during the break-in period. The guy who buys it when you're through with it may be barefooted and unable to pay for fixing it up.

9

How to Drive Fast

SPORTS CARS MUST BE DRIVEN. IF YOU WANT A plush automaton, buy a Detroit product. If you really like to drive, get a sports or competition car. Drivers' cars run all the way from just a sporty companion to a sizzling hot babe with a wildcat's temperament demanding constant attention and great skill to control.

Whatever type it is, the design of any competition car makes it safer at highway speeds than the typical sloppy American family sedan. But these very factors can also make it a much more dangerous car. Like the hockey player, it is a specialist in quick cornering, spinning, and fast stopping; these things give the *experienced* driver complete control in emergency situations. The competition car becomes dangerous, however, especially to the newcomer, when he overtaxes its road-holding ability.

The driver who has just switched over from domestic machinery is usually amazed at first how much faster he can take familiar turns, whip through traffic, and stop on a mosquito's head. If he is the first of his group to own a sports car, he will quite likely want to give every one of his friends a personal frame-twisting demonstration. It is also quite possible that, in his enthusiasm, he will try turns and bends at speeds that would make professional race drivers turn ashen. If our novice has lost his rabbit's foot, he may very well end up a vital statistic.

Learning by Watching

One of the very best ways to learn any sport is to *watch.* It might pay good dividends to join the best sports car club available and attend all of its events. At all club meets there will be two types of drivers performing. The most impressive (and the one who demands the most attention) is the grandstander who unnecessarily burns rubber and slides all over the course. Spectacular acrobatics are usually the mark of a lousy driver.

The one to study is the driver who regularly wins or finishes very close. He is seldom noticed by the crowd until the announcer says he is leading the race. Just as good swimmers look effortless and a Davis Cup ranker seems to cover the tennis court with ease, ace drivers rarely abuse a car. They position their mounts so well for making turns that they appear to be only half-trying. Road aces figure ahead—how long their tires will last, and so on—and they ration the amount of hard sliding they will do, depending on the length of the race.

When the beginner has seen one or two races, preferably from a tight curve, he is now ready to learn, himself—*not* how to race, but the essentials of good driving. The first step is to buy a good car; for the beginner I would suggest an MG, Triumph, or Morgan.

With these cars it is possible to pull every clunker in the book without killing anybody. But always remember, people can get killed in these cars, too.

Perhaps the best way to get started would be for you to level with a big sports car dealer who handles many makes. You can explain that this is your first attempt and get the dealer to promise to have someone teach you how to handle the car, if you buy one.

Nearly every foreign sports car dealer in the country has an expert demonstrator. Fellows who are "really gone" on the sport often try to make their living by selling cars. The prospective customer can get one of them to show off happily on the road and explain how to corner, brake, and shift gears. If the neophyte is smart enough to ooze with respect, the semi-pro will bubble with information and reveal every trick he has up his sleeve.

The danger in learning to drive a sports or competition car cannot be over-emphasized, and the writer accepts no responsibility in the event of any accident. These are merely suggestions. The writer does *not* recommend anyone becoming a race driver, since he feels this is strictly for the birds. But if you are a bird, let's go.

Learning by Driving

When the new sports car owner has his car home he is really out to learn. With the information he has gained from the dealer's "Stirling Moss" he must perfect his shifting and timing by himself. This can be a very expensive lesson, but definitely one that can't be by-passed. Fortunately, many race cars now have synchromesh transmissions that do not demand the double-clutching required of old, but there are still jobs around that must be double-clutched.

Shifting and Timing

Shifting gears quickly one way or the other is a matter of timing and coordination, and nothing else. Learning to slam-shift *up* is easy enough, but coming *down* (unless you have synchromesh) is quite a trick —one only lots of experience and chipped gear teeth will teach, if you expect to be really fast.

The rpm on a sports car tachometer are the shifting payoff. In road-racing or hill-climbing, the higher the rpm are kept, the more power and efficiency comes from the engine. When rpm start to fall off because of, let's say, a grade, this is the crucial point. Horsepower is being lost, and an immediate shift to a lower gear is indicated to keep the rpm and the power at peak. With synchromesh it will become evident (by keeping the throttle flat to the floor and throwing out the clutch) that, in the instant of lag, the rpm have picked up enough (through the relief of engine load) to allow slamming into a lower gear without any grinding. The action on most cars is almost instantaneous.

Double-clutching for non-synchromesh transmissions (such as in Ferraris, etc.) calls for a different technique. Two lightning jabs of the clutch pedal—with the final thrust of your hand-shift made at the instant your foot goes down for the second time—is double-clutching.

For cars that *must* be double-clutched, the student should get an expert to demonstrate, thereby saving expensive repair bills. The ability to reduce gears fast has two important payoffs. First, it helps build up speed instantly on getting around a turn. Second, the lower gears give more power, torque and pickup to get the car under control in a slide, skid, or other tight spot. This can be called "rear-wheel steering."

Transmissions come cheaper in the cheaper cars, which is another reason why they are best to learn in. The newcomer to sports car racing must learn to become an expert "box-boy," as they say in Umbrella Land, before he can even consider competition. No written word will tell him how. The art must be learned the hard way, and it's good business for the transmission companies.

Cornering and Slides

For learning to corner and to control slides and spins, a large open space is essential. In nearly every section of the country a deserted airport (or a little-used one) can be found. This is one of the best places to learn. Another good spot, if you don't get thrown off, is a huge parking lot at a race track or amusement park in off-seasons.

The space is needed to learn just how far slides will carry, and just how much steering control there is at different speeds. If this is tried on a deserted road, the road might suddenly not be wide enough for a slide or a hard cornering maneuver and, without the room to make mistakes, the driver might end up dead (from a roll-over) before he even got started. The wide airports, with hundreds of feet on either side of a runway, will allow one to counter-control if the car feels as though it is wheel-lifting. An old dirt or sand track is the best place to get the "feel" for slides and spins; a concrete runway has a way of holding too hard at times, and can't offer the "feel" of soft dust under the wheels.

In every section of the country there are still a lot of dirt roads that are good for learning necessary wheel and steering control. On these deserted roads and on wet, oily parking lots (especially those with asphalt surfaces), it is possible to learn how to control a skid by cutting the wheels into it; and, also, just when it might be better to cut *away* from the skid to cause the car to spin. The new driver will also learn in this way how he can control skids and spins to a large degree by jumping on the throttle, and when not to.

Fifty million written words can never take the place of a few hours behind the wheel learning car control. You can't teach swimming in a bath tub—you have to almost drown a few times. All I hope to do is to give the freshman sports car driver or potential race driver a few thoughts he must work out for himself.

Start off on soft dust or dirt, if possible, with gentle slides. To do this, reduce gears correctly, hit the brakes *gently,* and cut the wheels *slightly.* This will cause the rear wheels to slide or skid. To get out of this slide, quickly cut the front wheels back toward the direction the skid is taking the car. By doing so, you will be snapped back on course with the car under control.

The driver will soon gain confidence as he starts to get the "feel" of skids and slides under nearly every condition. Control and counter-control start to come automatically, so that when a car goes into a skid or slide the driver can command it back onto a straight line with authority.

A slide is usually considered a purposeful skid. In racing, the biggest use for a slide is to get around corners and bends in the least possible time and land in the best position for running the next leg. Slides range from gentle rear-wheel slipping to the full "broadslide," which means the car is sliding at right angles to the road.

A gentle rear-wheel slide to the right or left can usually be started with a quick cut of the steering wheel. To increase a slide, barrel the engine and increase the wheel cut. Of course, when this is carried too far there is danger of a roll-over. The severity of the steering wheel cut and the amount of rear-wheel spin will determine the car's course.

A hard brake slide, used sometimes in tight corners, and sometimes to avoid obstructions on the course, is the same as a power slide except the brakes are applied and there is no rear-wheel spinning. This is the most dangerous type of slide, as it invites immediate roll-over if the road surface is bumpy or hard.

Usually a brake slide is instantly followed up with rear-wheel power before the car rolls. In this maneuver the driver hits the brakes, gets the car sliding and then barrels the engine to control forward traction. To get out of any slide, use the common skid tactics of quickly cutting the front wheels back toward the direction of the slide.

Spinning a car is an advanced slide that carries further than right-angle travel. To spin a car, the same tactics are used as in bringing a car into a slide, then carried beyond by barreling the engine a bit while cutting the steering wheel back. The main purpose of a spin is to avoid crack-ups on a blocked course. In some cases, where turns are extreme, a three-quarter spin is used by the experts to get around the corner and into the correct next-leg position faster.

The spin can range from a 180-degree reverse-course whirl to a full 360-degree turn. Some drivers have used spin tactics in emergencies where regular braking would not have been adequate to avoid a crash, and where the chance on a spin was better than heading off-course into a stone wall or deep ditch. Spinning is also called "rear-wheel steering," and it is one of the most important tricks in the expert's book.

When the student has slides and spin control down cold, he may try rounding imaginary corners and continuing on, just as though he were in a race. An airport or huge empty parking lot is almost essential for this, because if the student tries it on an actual road he might flip into a ditch or slam into a telephone pole long before he was ready for such a confined maneuver.

With lots of space around, such as an airport usually affords, the student can go off his imaginary road time and again without damage. He will soon recognize the importance of all the previous practice as he realizes he can get around corners with less car lean if he barrels around using the power of the rear outside wheel as a stabilizer. On a hard turn, the inside wheel is usually free-wheeling, and the outside one, which is going faster, has all the power and lift to help fight rolling over or going off the course.

As the driver progresses he will learn to depend more and more on the outside rear wheel to get him around and control spins—so here comes another warning: some imported sports cars with bantam-size engines haven't enough torque to provide any rear-wheel help. For them, most of this type of driving is limited. Rear-wheel high-torque driving calls for a powerful engine.

Big-car Driving

Big-car driving is a horse of another color—and twice as dangerous. When a driver is slamming around a curve at close to a hundred and finds the car holding the road, that's one thing—if it lets go, that's another. The man who has had a lot of small car racing under his belt before going into big cars has some advantage under some circumstances, and absolutely none under others.

With 250 horsepower or more under the hood of a comparatively light sports car, the experienced driver has an additional high torque control factor to get him out of a pinch. This factor is not available to the man driving a low-powered car. The big-car man deals in power *versus* inertia. To get around any curve or bend at high speeds, when momentum tends to lead us straight ahead, extreme power is needed at the rear wheel to maintain traction and shift the polar axis of inertia from one direction to another.

On a hard curve at high speeds, all the engine power obtainable is needed on the outside rear wheel (the power wheel on curves with cars using a conventional differential) to lift against and fight the force that would roll the car off the road. As O'Toole, the hysterical embalmer might say, "What a spot to run out of fuel!"

Oddly enough, there are curves that can be taken at 100 mph or better but not at 80. Track drivers have often experienced this on highly-banked corners. This condition does exist on some curves, but should be left to the experts only. It's like the "G" force which enables a pail full of water to be swung in a full circle without spilling.

It works something like this. On some race circuits there occur slight turns, or "S" bends, that are simple to get around at speeds up to 70 mph. At perhaps 90, this simple curve is a killer. Forward speed is not enough to compensate the straight-line driving inertia that is causing a four-wheel drift off the road, so the driver gets killed.

If the car had been driven 25 mph faster, at 115 mph, the extra force, speed and power might have gotten it right around that turn as if in a groove. The inertia that killed the driver by causing the car to slide wouldn't even have had a chance to develop at 25 mph faster because the forward driving power and speed would have had the car past the bad spot before the polar movement of inertia (by the slight change of course) could take over in a slide.

This is stuff for the professional only. These are the problems the expert continental drivers of the thirties had to investigate, since it was their bread and butter, but *please,* don't *you* try it! (My readers are the most important people in the world to me.) These continental drivers all had team captains or managers who walked every foot of every course they were to drive, making notes on pitch and angles of approach. After much study, then, and then *only,* was any attempt ever made to fight extreme slide inertia with extreme power and speed.

Learning How Not *to Race*

Go to a road race and watch the experts get into and out of hard turns without effort, and then watch the show-offs, slamming and skidding, throwing rubber far and wide. The grandstander unnecessarily menaces every thing and person on the course. This type of driving unfortunately often impresses newcomers to the sport who don't know enough to see the abusive side of such car handling.

I remember one young driver fresh out of college who had just finished his first big road race a couple of days before. Someone else mentioned one of our best drivers and consistent performers. The youngster immediately jumped in with both feet, saying in effect, "He slows way down for every turn, so much so he's hard to pass on a corner—why, he's just a stick-in-the-mud." This young man had almost demolished his car in the fifth lap when he spun out and rolled over. The man he was criticizing finished second.

In the sports car circuit there are some remarkably good drivers and some old-timers who really make fools out of the grandstanders at times. The expert has learned through pre-race practice runs just how fast every corner should be hit. If it calls for a close inside cut, as on an "S" bend, he will carry his duel with the ham right up to the bend, only *he* will be on the inside. The grandstander, if he's a real ham, will usually refuse to drop back to get on the inside too, because he'll lose his passing position, and will try to take the bend at much too high a speed on the outside. *SCReeeeeeeeeeeeeCH!* Scratch one novice.

Brainy, tactical driving separates the men from the boys. No race was ever won on the first lap, and no race was ever won by a car that didn't finish.

Braking

Another major difference between sports and conventional cars is braking. All road-race aces save their brakes as much as possible, because when they *have* to use them the braking action is severe and overuse might cause "brake fade."

Brake fade is very common in course racing and is caused by the brake drums becoming distorted from too much heat. This momentary distortion prevents the brake shoes from gripping the brake drums, which can be very unhealthy. Usually there is no warning. After a few hard-braked turns the driver might find himself unable to stop. Quick brake jabs will keep the brakes cooler than a long, hard push.

In an emergency though, when he *must* stop, the correct braking method is a good solid, steady push. Don't let the wheels lock and skid, as this is *not* the fastest way to stop. The fastest way is to keep the wheels just on the point of locking, but still turning. Remember, in hard braking at high speeds there is always a good chance that if the front wheels lock, the car will tip and somersault. At the slightest indication of this let off on the brake and try again.

High-speed Driving

Although spins, slides, and correct braking require hours of dangerous practice, alert, fast reaction time is a prerequisite for high-speed driving. Many people think there is not too much skill required to drive wide-open in a straight line, other than to keep the foot throttle down. High-speed driving, especially over 100 mph, can be dangerous for a number of unexpected reasons.

Check your reaction time, because it varies from day to day. A variation of 1/10 of a second is far too much. Just 2/100 of a second can mean life or death at high speeds, especially in racing. Take a regular 1/100 of a second stop watch (a 1/10 of a second watch *won't* do) and hold it in the palm of your hand with your trigger finger on the winding and starting stem. Start the watch by squeezing, just like squeezing the trigger of a gun, release, then see how fast you can push the stem again. The average for three tries should be 16/100's or better —20/100's is much too slow.

When something out of the ordinary occurs at really high speeds, the driver must exercise a masterful bit of underplaying. A three-inch cut of the wheel of a fast car, wide-open, can start it into a 1,000-foot somersault.

Rosemeyer, the great German Auto-Union driver, was killed when his car passed several small trees on the Autobahn. There was about a five mph crosswind blowing when he started his speed run. The Auto-Union was bowling along at open throttle with the front wheels cut just enough to counteract the slight crosswind. When the trees were passed, the wind was broken. This caused Rosemeyer to shoot off the road, because his wheels were still cut to allow for the breeze. At 200 mph he was off the road before he could counter-correct.

Cross-currents and even scattered clouds can make

high-speed driving extremely dangerous. Trees and buildings near the road are treacherous, because, if there is a wind blowing, they can set up weird currents that can get you to the pearly gates before you can say "ouch."

Another dangerous condition at high speed is a road slick caused by a puddle of water or oil. If this allows traction to be broken on one wheel for just an instant, it can throw the car off balance. The experienced driver takes all this into consideration and is constantly prepared for a counter-control movement. The guy who drives with one hand at speeds above 100 mph is just waiting for the devil to stamp his application blank.

During all these practice sessions the driver should wear a safety belt and crash helmet. If he feels the car is going over and out of control, he should head for the cellar, *quick*. This means to get as much of the driver as possible under the instrument panel, and the rest of his body on the floor. Professionals practice this maneuver by the hour. Some shoulder safety belts make this a hard deal, but with the regular waist belt (*properly installed on the car frame*) the chauffeur can get most of himself below the doorline, where he won't be crushed. The moment the car stops, he should crawl out, since it may catch fire instantly.

When the race fledgling has all these lessons down pat, he might take to the deserted back roads and gently try some control driving there. He should go to the next sports car event and watch the experts again, asking himself if he does everything they do on various turns and corners. If the answer is "Yes," then he may be ready to enter a novice event for experience.

10

How to Drive in Competition

SPORTS CAR RACING IN AMERICA HAVING BECOME a major sport (as proven by 100,000-plus attendance at a number of scheduled events throughout the country), it's time to be concerned with the special driving techniques it requires. Sports car road racing in the U.S. dwindled from the old Vanderbilt Cup days to a complete fade-out during the Depression. In Europe, road racing has never ceased being *the* major sport.

Road-race Drivers

A brand-new generation of American road-race enthusiasts, in just a few short years following World War II, not only built new cars, but have produced drivers who have gotten more than just a foot in the doorway of European supremacy. On the Continent, before World War II, such factory teams as Mercedes, Auto-Union, and Alfa-Romeo actually ran race-driving schools. Their top team drivers drove thousands of miles each year in company practice cars on synthetic —and real—race circuits. Old timers, such as Mercedes' Neubauer, a former driver and after World War II the John J. McGraw of race team managers, spent hundreds of hours with each of his drivers. He showed them how to make the most speed through corners, how to handle a slide or spin to advantage, and how to conserve brakes. These men were trained with all the care of a heavyweight fighter seeking the world's championship. Today in Europe high speed road driving is considered a fine and exacting profession.

In the United States our expert drivers were just a group of greenhorn amateurs, for the most part. Nearly all our present top crop got their start driving ineffectual small cars on poorly-controlled amateur circuits. Most of these men had jobs, or were in businesses that occupied their time five days or more every week. The only time available for their sport was an occasional weekend club meet. Unlike their European counterparts, who made racing a profession, our drivers can more accurately be classified as hobbyists with a yen for good automobiles.

The deeper you look into what they had to work with, the more you appreciate the degree of skill our drivers have developed. In Europe, the average top driver learned how to drive in cars that were correctly suspended and balanced, and steered like automobiles. In America, nearly every one of our boys did his first wheel-turning or made his first automotive solo in a Detroit side-wheeler that handled with all the ease of a lapful of ice cubes.

On second thought, however, maybe our Detroit pogo-sticks could take actual credit for the way Americans learned to drive sports cars so quickly. Did you ever see a batter in a big-league game swinging three or four bats before he steps to the plate? It makes handling the single bat so much easier when facing the pitcher. Well, driving many of our Detroit products is similar to swinging four bats. After learning on these, a real sports car seems like a maiden's dream of being marooned on an island with a regiment of Marines.

Naturally, the sports car buyer who has no intention of racing doesn't need all this training. It might be wise, though, for his own pleasure, to learn a few medium-light power slides at reasonable speeds. Learning to control skids and how to maneuver in a tight spot could easily save his life, even on a sedately paced and controlled parkway.

The Basic Requirements

Automobile racing is a dangerous game. In no other sport does the beginner find such an excellent opportunity to have himself sawed in two and end up in an early grave. By the same token, in no other sport does the expert stand such an excellent chance of losing his life at the hands of amateurs. The toughest question is how to become an expert competition driver without getting thoroughly stiff from embalming fluid first.

Before going any further, I want to repeat that I don't recommend road racing as a healthy pastime. In fact, I do not recommend anyone entering any automotive competition of any kind, aside from rallies. All I can hope to do is suggest some ways of learning how to get the most out of a sports car and, I hope, stay alive.

Timing is the most important single quality a good competition driver must have. It's something that cannot be taught. The ability to cope with split-second emergencies through hyper-fast physical and mental reactions is an absolute *must*. Most star athletes make good drivers because their sense of timing is tops. If a man is a duffer on the golf course, dances like a three-legged giraffe, and swims like an oil-soaked ostrich, then the chances are he'd better forget competition driving.

If he has been a goon at sports all his life and is generally considered awkward, he should not plan on using his car for road racing or he will most likely end up a casualty—and he may take some good drivers with him. If he is prone to blowing his top in a pinch and is subject to good judgment blackouts when the chips are down and his (or someone else's) life is at stake, then sports car racing is definitely not for him. If he gets physically exhausted in a matter of minutes under a strain, and if he finds he can't be alert and relaxed while flirting with Lady Death, he should give up all thoughts of road racing.

The ability to relax and the ability to face almost certain extinction in a tight spot without becoming panicky is another definite must, if he is ever to become a top-flight race pilot. Few men have all these qualities to the full measure, but those who do are the men who become champions.

Lightning coordination is another must. Arms, legs, and all muscles must work simultaneously, without the slightest pause, when the brain commands. A pause of 1/10 of a second in reaction can easily spell curtains. If a man doesn't possess all the qualities above, but does possess most of them, he may still get some pleasure out of small-car inter-club racing. If he is considering big-league racing he should possess *all* of these qualities. Otherwise, he endangers not only his own life, but the lives of everyone else on the course.

So let's assume the man this is written for is the local golf champ and Fred Astaire of the country club, and that he just wants a few tips on how to become another Phil Hill.

No one with less than 50,000 miles on the old Detroit chrome-barge should even consider buying a sports car for competition. In spite of all the nasty things written about them by myself and others, family cars do provide basic training similar to ground school for flying. After 50,000 miles of driving anything, a certain feeling for steering is unconsciously picked up.

Braking and cornering are also absorbed to a degree. If the neophyte is an old hand at racing cars on a track, he may have a slight edge, but not too much. Many great professional track drivers with wins at Indianapolis have proven themselves the rankest of amateurs at road racing, and not much better in American stock cars. Road or stock-car racing is an entirely different game, and calls for an entirely different technique from race-car track driving.

Types of Competition Drivers

There are a variety of driving and racing technicians. First, there is the "killer" driver who is a specialist at pressing a car far beyond the point that it is normally expected to go. The "killer" is not a car nor equipment saver, but will, when the occasion warrants it, literally rip the tires and chassis apart and press the engine to the bursting point in order to snatch a win from a failure position. If he is on a team, at the captain's order, the "killer" will set a pace that will blow up the opposing hot-shots. All the good continental teams have "killer" drivers as standard equipment.

In addition to the "killer" there is the "winner." Most of the world's great drivers (including our own) are capable of being "killers" *or* "winners" at the flick of a pit signal. A "winner" driver must be capable and talented enough to maintain the maximum speed possible with a minimum of car abuse and risk.

The "winner" watches his instruments like a hawk at all times for signs of over-extending trouble. He has developed a gift for going through corners and bends with the smoothness of hair oil flowing over a bald head. He must also know every tactical trick in the book, and how to avoid being sucked into pitfalls on bad turns by the "killer" drivers.

Last, but far from least, is the "finisher." "Finisher" drivers nearly always finish, and nine times out of ten they finish in the money. Such men never abuse a car beyond the point of necessity, whether working alone or on a team. The "finisher" drivers are not always used by continental teams. Where they are not used, disaster often results in complete failure.

Oddly enough, however, after studying the world's best drivers for many years, I am forced to conclude that drivers, like leopards, can't change their spots. A "killer" *always* drives like a "killer." The "winner" driver comes the closest to being versatile. He can, on occasion, drive both ways. The "finisher" rarely changes, but he finishes in the money consistently.

To borrow a phrase from General MacArthur, "There is no substitute for victory." While you need the balance of different driving skills, you also need, as in most sports, a team manager who has an instinct for timing men and machines. He has nothing to do with actual driving in the race, but if you are going to learn to drive and want to race, you might as well win. This man may be hated or worshiped by the crew, but he *must* be respected. Whether he is a "Good Joe" or a big bully, if he doesn't know his business his team is licked before it starts. Neubauer is the classic example of the perfect team manager.

The Single Entry

The single entry in any sports car race rarely has a Neubauer to guide him. He doesn't have a teammate to help him blow off the opposition. If the single entry is out to win, he will have to take all the team factors into consideration and pinpoint them on himself. After a few rounds of practice on the course to be raced, he will soon determine, with the aid of his pit crew and their stop-watches, the maximum speed he can safely negotiate the course and the fastest speed he can get around and still finish with original rubber, or a minimum of pit stops.

On the typical American feature race course of 200 miles or less, one pit stop is usually all that is needed to lose a race. Amateur pit crews are usually very amateurish, indeed. Their intentions may be great, but the typical amateur becomes all thumbs the moment he has to change a tire, unstrap a hood to add oil, or even clean the windshield. What might be only a temporary loss of a few positions with a professional crew may turn into a fast trip to the cellar with well-meaning, untrained amateurs.

For this reason, unless the race is an endurance event, it is usually wiser for the American sports car racer to set a far slower pace if it means he can avoid one pit stop. If a set of tires will last out an entire 200-mile race at an average speed of 75 mph, this might prove a lot smarter than burning up rubber at an 80 mph clip, if the faster pace would involve several additional pit stops for new rubber or water. The time consumed in slowing down to make the stop and then getting away again can be slightly less agonizing than a broken neck.

Anyone can look good driving superior equipment. Unfortunately, in many races in this country there is always some outstanding equipment handled by professional-amateurs racing as a team that make it pretty tough for the single entry to crash through. The equipment is usually more uniform in the preliminary races for production cars, divided into classes either by price or engine displacement.

Since it is almost impossible to win a feature event of any major American sports car race without a 100 per cent professional crew, let's consider ways of winning a production class race.

Once you have determined your maximum permissible speed and your maximum emergency sprint speed, here is some typical strategy. Assuming that your car is tuned to the teeth (and you have no right to race unless it is), you might rightly take the tack that since this is a *production* car race, all the cars in the event will be equally fast, give a mile or two one way or the other (see Chapter 14).

It is up to you now to try to outsmart your opponents before the race begins—to determine just how close you can guess the breaking point of your tires, the fade-out of your brakes, and the blow-up point of your engine. If you could figure this exactly 1000 per cent right, the moment you crossed the finish line your tires would blow out, the engine would blow up and you'd be out of brakes!

As you can see, it is quite similar to running a horse in the Kentucky Derby—never *all* the way out and never too slow, but just right—to keep the glue factory agents off your neck.

As already stated, there are two ways of running in a race like this. The surest way is to win it as *slowly* as you can. In a race with 20 cars (not professionally driven) you can usually count that 25 per cent of the drivers will be prototype maniacs. With the starting signal, they will go all-out, taking corners too fast, burning rubber and brakes idiotically. Half of these will end up off the course, in haybales, upside-down, and so on. The other, luckier half will just have engines that catch fire or freeze, brakes that disappear, and tires that explode.

This leaves 75 per cent of the field still running. The leader (who we hope will be you) has paced himself to the 1/1000 and is now beginning to reap the harvest of wisdom.

At the starting signal, you've jumped into first place as soon as you could and have become the leader. On typical American race courses, and on some airport circuits, being in the lead has a tremendous advantage. You and you alone have your choice on how to approach every corner and you and you alone can set the pace on how fast these corners will be taken. Without meaning a pun—you are in the driver's seat.

The only way you can be passed is in a straightaway or by very clever maneuvering by an opponent in a corner. Actually, if you know your cornering and competition technique you can never be passed in a typical corner by anyone driving a car of equal speed. Naturally, you must anticipate some sharp moves from behind, but if you're on the ball, *you* have control of the race. From this position you can actually save your car in the corners, but your opponents will force you to a maximum of acceleration, and to top speed on the straights.

Let's assume that you are in the unlucky second spot and old meany Herman Glockenfeather, taking the full sweep of every turn (which is pretty narrow to start with), is keeping you right in your place. You both accelerate at about the same clip, and you both have about the same top speed—so how can you pass him?

There are several ways you might do it, if Herman isn't as sharp as a new tack. You might make a feinting pass several times on the outside, which he cuts off at the last minute by letting his car drift further to the outside.

Winning Chrysler 300 gets checkered flag at beginning of one-mile standing start at Daytona Beach.

A machine of which Detroit can justly be proud, the Corvette, gets the flag as it trips the magic eye in the foreground during a run over Daytona's Measured Mile.

Oldtime Veritas, powered by a Corvette engine, digging away fast enough to win the sports car division of the standing-start mile at Daytona.

Bill France, czar of stock car racing, poses with the author before the start of a race. France in 1959 completed building the world's fastest track, 2½ miles long, at Daytona Beach.

Classic, twenty-year-old SS-100.

From a purely aesthetic standpoint, nothing built in the world today can compare with the stately leviathans of a quarter century ago. This Hispano-Suiza, 6,000 pounds of glamor, is one of the real classics of the Twenties and Thirties.

Racing a 1901 steam-driven Locomobile with tiller controls.

A 1902 right-hand-drive Maxwell leads a procession of antique cars from the Wichita, Kansas airport.

Your used sports car may or may not have had the loving attention this racing machine is getting just before the 24-Hours at LeMans.

Supremely worthy of this regal No. 7 Maserati, and the covey of haughty Ferraris in the rear, are their four-figure repair bills.

Rear view of burned-out Porsche Carrera: the result of too much speed and not enough cooling.

Your sports car isn't ready for cornering like this until after many miles of careful breaking in.

Bending a top-flight 3.4 Jag.

This MG at New Smyrna Beach, Florida, demonstrates the hard way to get around a corner. Note roll bar behind driver's head, which undoubtedly saved him from serious injury. After this roll, the car continued and finished the race.

72

When discretion is the better part of valor: aim straight off the course (provided there's no ditch or obstructions) rather than risk a rollover by trying to take the bend at excessive speed.

England's pride and joy, balding, lantern-jawed Stirling Moss, who drives in ballet slippers and is the equal of Babe Ruth on the Tight Little Isle. Here he's seen yakking with reporter before a race.

Serious competition requires every ounce of the parts and equipment jammed into this VW Kombi in the foreground and into the Fruehauf trailer to the rear.

This small team operation gets by with a modest station wagon for its mobile parts house.

Like beetle shells abandoned by their inhabitants, these Lotus bodies wait outside the team garage at Sebring while chassis get a last-minute check: another part of extensive pre-race preparations.

Then on the seventh or eighth try you might start this same old feint again to the outside, only this time you have reduced gears a notch. You slap your brake just for an eye-blink with a sharp wheel-cut to the right and barrel the engine so that you just miss his tail whipping back toward the inside, and *away* you *go*, running right up inside of him.

This *might* just work, but the odds are against you if Herman is sharper than a blunt instrument. Anyway, it should make Herman nervous and even if he cuts this one off in time, if you keep mixing up your bids he may goof and you are through.

One of the best ways of causing Herman to goof is another tactic that calls for a little *guts.* If Herman won't let you through, start riding his tail as close as two feet at times and *stay* there down every straightaway and through every turn. Every time he glances in his rear mirror, there's your big, ugly snout waiting to jump right into his trunk at any moment.

I have seen some of the greatest drivers in the world break down when this tactic is used (including a World's Champion Grand Prix driver). It takes a man with iron nerves to withstand this threatening menace that he knows will crush him if he should go into a spin or be forced to use his brakes.

Usually (or eight times out of ten), the driver getting this treatment gets going too fast and spins out or just backs off and lets the trunk-eater get by. Such a maneuver calls for a lot of nerve on the part of the driver doing the forcing, but in amateur circles it is almost always 100 per cent effective.

When our boy was in Glockenfeather's position and leading, having read this book he knew the cure (which also takes a lot of nerve). He merely flipped his mirror up so he couldn't *see* his opponent behind him, and continued to take every corner just as it should be taken. There is only one right way to take any given corner at a given speed. Three feet to the right or three feet to the left is wrong, and not as fast as the right groove.

The third and last way to try to overcome the guy ahead rarely works, but it *has* worked. Start slowing down and let him get a quarter mile ahead of you if necessary. In order to save his car, the leading driver will gladly reduce his pace, too. After you have almost lulled him to sleep with a few of these slow laps and have him taking the corners like a Wayne King waltz, you suddenly take the hardest corner—closing in fast at the last instant—and barrel around at just one notch short of roll-over pace. Since you are now moving much faster than he, you can therefore accelerate much faster.

If your opponent has eased off enough, you may catch him flat-footed with his rpm's down as he heads for the straight. If you manage to pull this trick off, it's worth the price of six Jaguars just to see his agonized expression as you ooze by. Rarely do races run this even, except in top circuits. If you are a good poker player in civilian life, with some psychological talents, and have learned to drive correctly, you may very well end up with a lot of silverware.

To get back to that corner business for just an instant. Every corner has its right and wrong groove. If you're not sure exactly where it is, watch some of the semi-pros in practice and check this time with a stop watch. After the expert has found the groove, he will make several laps, trying it for speed. If you're on hand to catch just where he is grooving you'll have two strikes on your amateur opponents who haven't done the same thing.

To win any race calls for a lot of luck and making fewer mistakes than your opponent. The fact that the car to be raced must be mechanically perfect goes without saying. In order to be assured of victory, in addition to luck you must have a reliable pit crew with an intelligent manager and you, yourself, should have all of the qualifications needed by a top competition driver.

As your experience increases, many races will actually become a lot easier and seem almost effortless. When things go wrong, such as an impromptu blow-out or an unavoidable spin, then, and then only, can you end up in the first slot by being letter-perfect, not only in your car handling, but in the guts department.

To beat superior equipment with an inferior car is the toughest task of all, and often impossible. However, if you are to do it, you can do it in only one way. You, your pit crew, and your strategy must be far superior to your better-mounted opponent. Remember, it *has* been done.

What Is This Thing Called Speed?

And now at the end of this long lesson, what is it that makes a man's eyes glaze with snow-madness and prepare to try the ascent of the peak that killed his brother—and will prove nothing? What is it that makes a man risk his neck in high-speed driving?

Speed in a fast car is a sensation impossible to describe accurately—just as no writer has ever had the power to describe exactly sound, or taste, or smell. To be sure, speed is a thrill, but an odd sort of a thrill—the faster you go, the odder the sensation gets.

When driving extremely fast in competition, such as in a race or speed trial, the driver fully realizes that his very life depends on dozens of factors that were not remotely present before he got up to speed. Death has a firm grip on his shoulder, and the slightest error of judgment or failure of equipment will make the driver and Death full partners instantly. A tire failure, steering connection mishap, or a piece of rutted road surface can stamp "*paid*" on the driver's life ticket in an eye-wink.

These facts are known to the driver and are a completion of his thrill—that unlisted thrill (or sensation) that has made man risk his life in many needless pursuits since the beginning of time. The bull fighter, the pylon flyer, and all others who tempt death ruthlessly know the meaning, though few can explain it. Death to the bull fighter is agonizingly slow compared to the zip, roll, and crash of the race driver.

When going into a corner fast you always ask yourself—what are my chances of getting around? The faster you go, the less the chance. But for thrills, eating up (in a four-wheel drift) the full bend of a turn, right to the last inch, before getting that "O.K.-you-made-it" feeling, is a thrill no one who has never experienced it will ever know.

Crazy? Definitely, but a lot of guys do it every weekend.

11

Hillclimbs, Trials, and Le Concours d'Elegance

SO MUCH FOR THE TOP-SEEDED ROAD RACE. THERE are other forms of competition in which men and machines can show their mettle, each requiring different talents and the mastery of special skills.

Possible runner-up in popularity to road racing, here and abroad, is the hillclimb, a great spectator sport which is lots of real fun for the driver. Basically, hillclimbs are simple. A steep slope is selected and the guy getting from the bottom to the top in the fastest time gets the crate of bananas. Naturally, the bigger of these events are run in many classes. In America, Pike's Peak is our most outstanding, but there are other, slightly lesser clambakes like the Mount Washington Hillclimb and the Devil's Despair reverse dip. In addition to these three uphill hikes, there are many regional and smaller events run throughout the year.

A good hillclimb usually calls for two distinct geographical features. First, the rise must be steep—the steeper the better—and second, it must contain a lot of turns and twists (which are the only factors that make hillclimbing sporty).

There is a definite technique required in these mountain-topping tussles that differs quite a bit from road racing. Usually these events are far less dangerous than out-and-out road racing because Old Man Gravity acts as an extra set of brakes to slow you down when biting into a corner too hard. However, it should always be borne in mind that you *can* cause a gleam in a buzzard's eyes by leaving the road, rolling, or crashing into some immovable object.

On many hillclimbs not even the most powerful cars ever get into top gear, so these competition hill-levelers usually have a lot more torque and dig at the rear wheels for corner control than cars running flat-out in top gear or coming down on their brakes for a flat turn. In one word, most hillclimbs can be summed up as a contest of *torque*—torque being the gutty quality in the power school that twists your rear wheels. Developed horsepower in a hillclimb is usually of little importance. Dig and acceleration are torque champs, and this is what is needed if you intend to drive home with a load of silverware.

As in road racing, there is no set formula for getting you around any corner or curve; everything depends on the particular corner or curve to be taken. It is rare, however, in hillclimbing, for a long-arc sweep to be the smartest tactic. Of course, the road surface plays a big part, but generally speaking, the safest way to take a corner at high speed when going uphill is usually to cut the inside of the sharpest point so close that you trim the grass with your inside wheels.

If the corner has a right-angle snap, or a real dog-in-the-manger bend, this inside-cornering technique allows you the whole width of the road for an outward drift, or for your rear end to slide out. Usually, when the corner comes up on an extremely steep grade, the car is already in one of its lower gears, which will, under ordinary circumstances, give the driver more control than a pristine virgin.

In the larger classes, where hundreds of foot-pounds of torque are unleashed on a small driving gear, it is quite possible to get more fouled up than a French political poster manufacturer. However, as we have already indicated in this epistle, no one short of a two-headed Harvard man should compete in one of these gasket blowers unless he has a great deal of experience under him; this being the case, he can pay for his own funeral.

The real fun in hillclimbing is most often had by the none-too-serious sect of the game. These drivers of the underpowered little warts can have just as much fun as the big-car drivers without the risk. Actually, in cars of low torque and small displacement, a guy would really have to *try* to get himself beyond the need-of-a-Band-Aid stage.

As in every other form of motoring sport, the best way to enter hillclimbs is after attending a few as a spectator. If you have the observation qualities of a bag of cement you will quickly get on to the techniques used by the better drivers. Hillclimbs can be a lot of fun, and most of them are one-day affairs where even the kiddies are welcome in the event they run short of haybales. What makes hillclimbs doubly safe over road racing is that they are solo events—only one car making the run at a time.

The Trials

To my way of thinking, a "trial" is one of the greatest sports car events of all, and, regrettably, one rarely run in America. A trial usually consists of a number of rugged sports car drivers and owners who really like to get away from the beaten path. These are sometimes called "Field Trials." The course is most often on some huge private estate, or, in England and Ireland, on public lands where there are a variety of earthy conditions and many places where no four-wheeled motor vehicle has ever traveled before. This calls for a lot of clearance and experience in rough going.

Rarely is anyone ever hurt in a trial, but usually several baths are in order to bring the participant back to normal. Also, there is rarely any major harm done to the car that can't be corrected with a hosing-off. For example, the first part of the course might be through a thick woods and then lead into a swamp. In these swampy or boggy areas snow tires are very helpful. After the swamp the course may tear across an open field, dodging rocks and chuck holes, and into another woods. There may be a small stream that you are required to ford, with a slimy bank to climb afterwards. The course may be five miles long or only a mile, but if it's done right, in the right terrain, there'll be loads of sport and enough laugh material to carry you on for many months.

In Europe, especially England and Ireland, they often use the same course year after year, and setting a course record is as important to these advocates as winning at Le Mans is to their higher-speeded brothers. No four-wheel-drive cars like the Jeep are allowed (which is only fair), but there are a number of sports cars that are more suited for this work than others. For example, in England there are many specials that are built just for trial work. In addition, there are many production cars that find their only claim to fame is their trial ability. The old TC MG was a great trial car, and so are the Dellow and Morgan. In this country the greatest trial car we ever built (unknowingly) was the Model A Ford, with enough clearance to run over a lion without touching.

There have been one or two trials run here at home, and I hope sincerely it catches on, since, in my book, it is just one more place where the sports car can shine above conventional frumps, and, by running in trials, it *is* a sports car.

Concours d'Elegance

The last sports car event we will mention is the Wax Derby. Many sports cars in America with less than 5,000 miles on them have over 100,000 miles of wax on their bonnets. These are the "cream-puffs," the "look-but-don't-touch" competitors.

At many large sports car events, a contest is conducted before the major race is run to determine the prettiest, the niftiest, the cleanest and the most unique powder-puff. A lot of guys I know would think nothing of going over the *under*side of a fender with a silk handkerchief, in case an insect had been indiscreet during their absence.

Some of these cars are real gutty barges that are owned by people who are more interested in the car's aesthetic side than its athletic prowess. This is a particularly jolly event for male spinsters and, believe it or not, a number of real men participate, too. Actually, it's similar to a dog show, where the owner doesn't give a damn if his Irish setter would have a heart attack at the sound of a gun, or at the sight of a mouse, providing he *looks* handsome enough to be voted the best-looking in the show. In a way, this event before the major race is like voting for the spectator with the prettiest tie before the Dempsey-Firpo fight.

There are some entrants in these events, though, to

whom I take my hat off. These are the men who, at great expense and effort, have restored some classic sports car to its original condition. Those who have restored the real ones of a bygone era deserve a lot of credit and our thanks. Without them many of these cars would only be memories.

Rallies

At the time I wrote "The Modern Sports Car," I thought it would be sufficient to include rallies in the chapter on hillclimbs and other minor events. Since that time, however, they have made such gains in popularity and prestige as to warrant a chapter all their own.

Rallies are somewhat like vacuum cleaner bags—they contain a mixture of ingredients. A rally is a competition which usually taxes the skill of the driver, plus the ability and brainwork of a navigator, added to some secret ingredients known as correct instruments, timepieces, maps, and a bucketful of perseverance. Rallies, like the circus, come in all sizes, from small Sunday-afternoon club events to be enjoyed by the entire family, down to the dead-serious big-time runs that involve several days through hazardous terrain and often through snow and ice.

Most rallies, whether big-time professionally-driven

jobs or Saturday-night soirees, have one purpose in mind, and that is to get from point "A" to point "B"—but rarely by the quickest route. The simpler Sunday-picnic rally, of which hundreds are held each year in various parts of the country, may be a treasure hunt, a puzzle, or a professional-type rally in which average speed to the thousandth of a mph is the all-important ingredient.

Picnic Rallies

The picnic rally might start off as follows: The driver and his navigator (quite often his wife) are told before the start that all will wind up at Joe's Chophouse on the old turnpike for dinner. Now, Joe's Chophouse may only be 20 miles away, but if the rally stewards are diabolical and mean enough, your course to Joe's may easily take in 150 miles of driving. As you approach the starting line (cars are started at intervals ranging from 30 seconds to five minutes), the starter may hand you an instruction sheet that reads, "Proceed to route 101 at average speed of 28.3 mph. Turn right and average 31.4 mph until you pass intersection with route 117." (There's a typical rally instruction sheet at the end of this chapter.) Anyway, to make this brief, at various spots are hidden unannounced check points where you may be flagged down to report, or just ignored as you drive by, but your exact time of passing has been carefully noted—you hope.

The whole object of this deal is that, during the afternoon on the 150-mile jaunt, you have been running from one point to another, trying to maintain the exact average called for in the instructions and end up at Joe's Chophouse at the exact second you're supposed to, in order to maintain, let's say, a 31.2 mph average for the whole route. On the face of it, this looks pretty easy. All you have to do is go like a bomb for 149.5 miles, pull over to the side of the road a half mile from Joe's, then restart your engine with stopwatch in hand and cross the line exactly on the nose. The gimmick is those nasty little people at the various check points who have carefully kept track of your progress. If you arrived at a checkpoint a minute early, for instance, you will be penalized so many points, and the same if you're that much late. When all the penalty points are added at the end of the rally, the guy with the fewest is usually declared the winner, unless there's a tie, and then a run-off is called for. On page 136 is a map of a typical rally, "The Schnook's Tour," conducted by the Brandywine Motorsport Club.

The Navigator

To maintain a close to accurate average of let's say 31.7 for six miles, 37.3 for eleven, etc., until the finish calls for a lot more equipment than a two-dollar watch and an over-casual odometer. It means that the navigator must be equipped with from one to several extremely accurate timepieces, a computer (which may be a circular rule made specially for rallies) or a slide rule, or an expensive mechanical or electrical computer that will give you your average at any given minute down to the hundredth. Besides this, you should have a clip board with plenty of paper and several pencils or ball point pens for making calculations.

On top of all this you must add one more factor—the navigator *must,* if he's to be helpful, have a slight working knowledge of arithmetic. Any way you slice it, in a rally the big brains of the partnership is the navigator—the driver merely has to be a good driver to be successful. The navigator, in addition to all the above-mentioned talents, must be fairly quick with his compu-

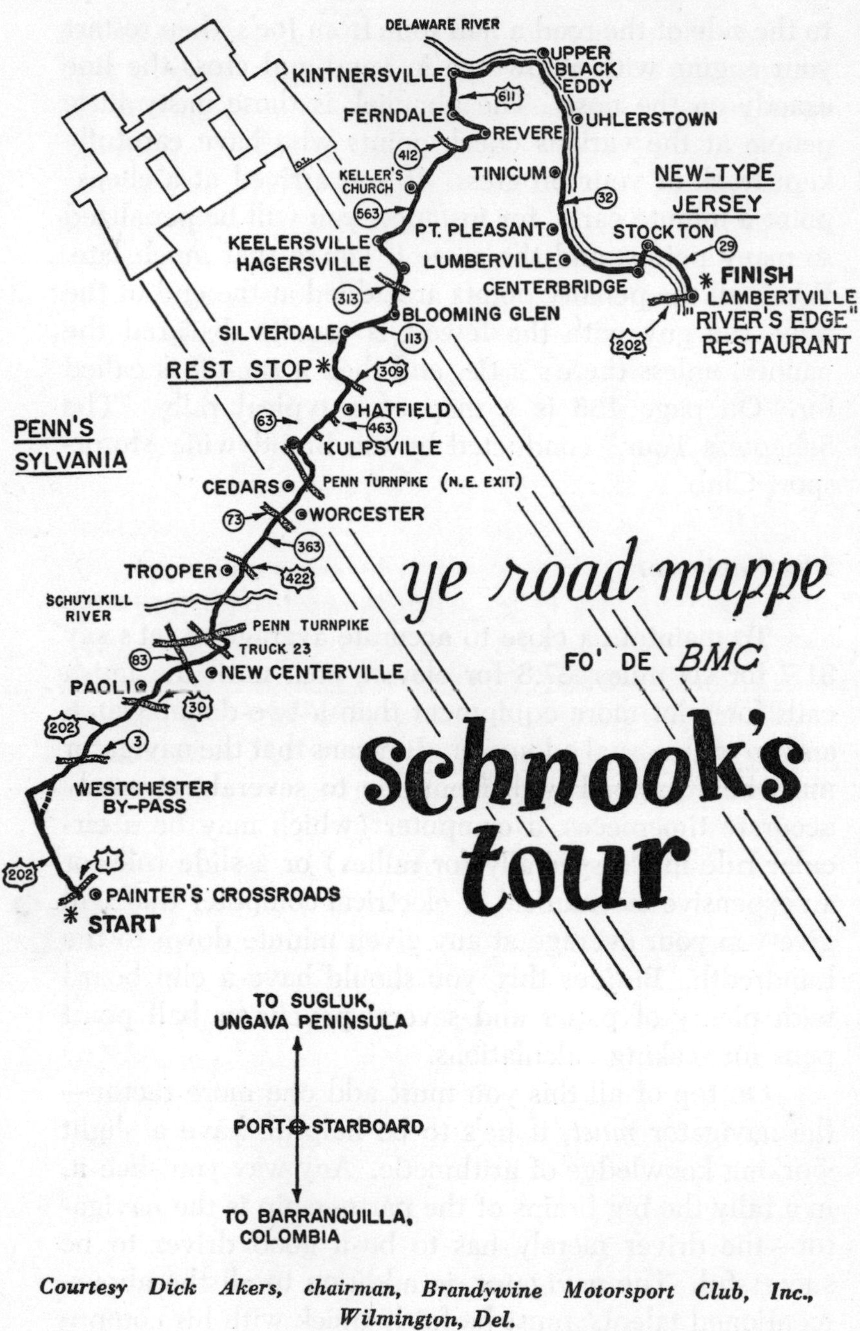

Courtesy Dick Akers, chairman, Brandywine Motorsport Club, Inc., Wilmington, Del.

tations. He relays the information to the driver as fast as possible—something like, "Pick it up, Herman, your average is a mile and a half slow." Or, "Knock it off, you're running three miles too fast, and there's probably some jerk around that next bend at a secret checkpoint." In the event there is (and there usually is), Herman had better pick up or drop his speed before rounding that bend. As an aid to navigators, we're including an invaluable table which permits you to determine the time it will take to cover a given distance at a given speed.

Puzzle Rallies

The puzzle, or treasure hunt, rallies are quite similar, but with an added ingredient, such as, "average 31.6 mph until you pass maple tree with broken limb, turn left at next dirt road and proceed by H. B. Hecker's mail box." If the guy laying out the rally is a real fiend, he may wait until he finds two adjoining farms owned by two brothers, and you may turn left at H. C. Hecker's instead of at H. B. Hecker's. Anyway, you get the point—good old clean dusty fun.

Treasure hunts may involve turning up at the finish with a copy of August 17th's *New York Times,* a bottle of Hockenglommer beer, or even a kitten. Sometimes a pair of pink bloomers may be demanded. No matter what it is the item is usually not easy to come by, and you all end up at old Joe's in hysterics and perhaps get arrested for drunken and malicious driving on the way home.

Classic Rallies

The big-time rallies, such as the Great American Mountain Rally, Alpine, or Monte Carlo, are less apt to

miles	miles per hour 15	16	17	18	19	20	21
0.1	00:24	00:23	00:21	00:20	00:19	00:18	00:1
0.2	00:48	00:45	00:42	00:40	00:38	00:36	00:3
0.3	1:12	1:08	1:04	1:00	00:57	00:54	00:5
0.4	1:36	1:30	1:25	1:20	1:16	1:12	1:0
0.5	2:00	1:53	1:46	1:40	1:35	1:30	1:2
0.6	2:24	2:15	2:07	2:00	1:54	1:48	1:4
0.7	2:48	2:38	2:28	2:20	2:13	2:06	2:0
0.8	3:12	3:00	2:49	2:40	2:32	2:24	2:1
0.9	3:36	3:23	3:11	3:00	2:51	2:42	2:3
1.0	4:00	3:45	3:32	3:20	3:10	3:00	2:5
2	8:00	7:30	7:04	6:40	6:19	6:00	5:4
3	12:00	11:15	10:35	10:00	9:29	9:00	8:3
4	16:00	15:00	14:07	13:20	12:38	12:00	11:2
5	20:00	18:45	17:39	16:40	15:48	15:00	14:1
6	24:00	22:30	21:11	20:00	18:57	18:00	17:0
7	28:00	26:15	24:43	23:20	22:07	21:00	20:0
8	32:00	30:00	28:14	26:40	25:16	24:00	22:5
9	36:00	33:45	31:46	30:00	28:26	27:00	25:4
10	40:00	37:30	35:18	33:20	31:35	30:00	28:3
11	44:00	41:15	38:50	36:40	34:45	33:00	31:2
12	48:00	45:00	42:22	40:00	37:54	36:00	34:
13	52:00	48:45	45:57	43:20	41:04	39:00	37:0
14	56:00	52:30	49:25	46:40	44:13	42:00	40:0
15	1:00:00	56:15	52:57	50:00	47:22	45:00	42:5
16	1:04:00	1:00:00	56:29	53:20	50:32•	48:00	45:4
17	1:08:00	1:03:45	1:00:00	56:40	53:42	51:00	48:3
18	1:12:00	1:07:30	1:03:32	1:00:00	56:51	54:00	51:2
19	1:16:00	1:11:15	1:07:04	1:03:20	1:00:00	57:00	54:1
20	1:20:00	1:15:00	1:10:36	1:06:40	1:03:10	1:00:00	57:0
21	1:24:00	1:18:45	1:14:08	1:10:00	1:06:19	1:03:00	1:00:0
22	1:28:00	1:22:30	1:17:40	1:13:20	1:09:29	1:06:00	1:02:5
23	1:32:00	1:26:15	1:21:11	1:16:40	1:12:38	1:09:00	1:05:4
24	1:36:00	1:30:00	1:24:43	1:20:00	1:15:48	1:12:00	1:08:3
25	1:40:00	1:33:45	1:28:15	1:23:20	1:18:57	1:15:00	1:11:2
26	1:44:00	1:37:30	1:31:47	1:26:40	1:22:07	1:18:00	1:14:
27	1:48:00	1:41:15	1:35:19	1:30:00	1:25:16	1:21:00	1:17:0
28	1:52:00	1:45:00	1:38:50	1:33:20	1:28:26	1:24:00	1:20:0
29	1:56:00	1:48:45	1:42:22	1:36:40	1:31:35	1:27:00	1:22:5
30	2:00:00	1:52:30	1:45:54	1:40:00	1:34:45	1:30:00	1:25:4
31	2:04:00	1:56:15	1:49:26	1:43:20	1:37:54	1:33:00	1:28:3
32	2:08:00	2:00:00	1:52:58	1:46:40	1:41:04	1:36:00	1:31:2
33	2:12:00	2:03:45	1:56:29	1:50:00	1:44:13	1:39:00	1:34:
34	2:16:00	2:07:30	2:00:00	1:53:20	1:47:22	1:42:00	1:37:0
35	2:20:00	2:11:15	2:03:32	1:56:40	1:50:32	1:45:00	1:40:0
36	2:24:00	2:15:00	2:07:04	2:00:00	1:53:42	1:48:00	1:42:5
37	2:28:00	2:18:45	2:10:36	2:03:20	1:56:41	1:51:00	1:45:4
38	2:32:00	2:22:30	2:14:08	2:06:40	2:00:00	1:54:00	1:48:3
39	2:36:00	2:26:15	2:17:40	2:10:00	2:03:10	1:57:00	1:51:2
40	2:40:00	2:30:00	2:21:11	2:13:20	2:06:19	2:00:00	1:54:
	15	16	17	18	19	20	21

22	23	24	25	26 (miles per hour)	27	miles
00:16	00:16	00:15	00:14	00:14	00:13	0.1
00:33	00:31	00:30	00:29	00:28	00:27	0.2
00:49	00:47	00:45	00:43	00:42	00:40	0.3
1:05	1:03	1:00	00:58	00:55	00:53	0.4
1:22	1:18	1:15	1:12	1:09	1:07	0.5
1:38	1:34	1:30	1:26	1:23	1:20	0.6
1:54	1:49	1:45	1:41	1:37	1:33	0.7
2:11	2:05	2:00	1:55	1:51	1:47	0.8
2:27	2:21	2:15	2:10	2:05	2:00	0.9
2:44	2:37	2:30	2:24	2:18	2:13	1.0
5:26	5:13	5:00	4:48	4:37	4:27	2
8:10	7:50	7:30	7:12	6:55	6:40	3
10:53	10:26	10:00	9:36	9:14	8:53	4
13:37	13:02	12:30	12:00	11:32	11:07	5
16:21	15:39	15:00	14:24	13:50	13:20	6
19:04	18:14	17:30	16:48	16:09	15:33	7
21:49	20:51	20:00	19:12	18:27	17:46	8
24:32	23:28	22:30	21:36	20:46	20:00	9
27:16	26:04	25:00	24:00	23:04	22:13	10
30:00	28:41	27:30	26:24	25:22	24:26	11
32:42	31:17	30:00	28:48	27:41	26:40	12
35:26	33:54	32:30	31:12	30:00	28:53	13
38:09	36:30	35:00	33:36	32:18	31:06	14
40:53	39:06	37:30	36:00	34:37	33:20	15
43:36	41:43	40:00	38:24	36:55	35:33	16
46:20	44:18	42:30	40:48	39:14	37:46	17
49:04	46:55	45:00	43:12	41:32	40:00	18
51:48	49:32	47:30	45:36	43:50	42:13	19
54:32	52:09	50:00	48:00	46:08	44:26	20
57:16	54:46	52:30	50:24	48:26	46:40	21
00:00	57:23	55:00	52:48	50:45	48:53	22
02:44	1:00:00	57:30	55:12	53:03	51:06	23
05:26	1:02:37	1:00:00	57:36	55:22	53:20	24
08:10	1:05:13	1:02:30	1:00:00	57:40	55:33	25
10:53	1:07:50	1:05:00	1:02:24	1:00:00	57:46	26
13:37	1:10:26	1:07:30	1:04:48	1:02:18	1:00:00	27
16:21	1:13:02	1:10:00	1:07:12	1:04:37	1:02:13	28
19:04	1:15:39	1:12:30	1:09:36	1:06:55	1:04:26	29
21:49	1:18:14	1:15:00	1:12:00	1:09:14	1:06:39	30
24:32	1:20:51	1:17:30	1:14:24	1:11:32	1:08:52	31
27:16	1:23:28	1:20:00	1:16:48	1:13:50	1:11:06	32
30:00	1:26:04	1:22:30	1:19:12	1:16:09	1:13:19	33
32:42	1:28:41	1:25:00	1:21:36	1:18:27	1:15:32	34
35:26	1:31:17	1:27:30	1:24:00	1:20:46	1:17:46	35
38:09	1:33:54	1:30:00	1:26:24	1:23:04	1:20:00	36
40:53	1:36:30	1:32:30	1:28:48	1:25:22	1:22:13	37
43:36	1:39:06	1:35:00	1:31:12	1:27:41	1:24:26	38
46:20	1:41:43	1:37:30	1:33:36	1:30:00	1:26:39	39
49:04	1:44:18	1:40:00	1:36:00	1:32:18	1:28:52	40
22	23	24	25	26	27	

miles	miles per hour 28	29	30	31	32	33	34
0.1	00:13	00:12	00:12	00:12	00:11	00:11	00:1
0.2	00:26	00:25	00:24	00:23	00:23	00:22	00:2
0.3	00:39	00:37	00:36	00:35	00:34	00:33	00:3
0.4	00:51	00:50	00:48	00:46	00:45	00:44	00:4
0.5	1:04	1:02	1:00	00:58	00:56	00:55	00:5
0.6	1:17	1:15	1:12	1:10	1:08	1:05	1:0
0.7	1:30	1:27	1:24	1:21	1:19	1:16	1:1
0.8	1:43	1:40	1:36	1:33	1:30	1:27	1:2
0.9	1:56	1:52	1:48	1:44	1:41	1:38	1:3
1.0	2:09	2:04	2:00	1:56	1:53	1:49	1:4
2	4:17	4:08	4:00	3:52	3:45	3:38	3:3
3	6:26	6:13	6:00	5:48	5:38	5:27	5:1
4	8:34	8:17	8:00	7:44	7:30	7:16	7:0
5	10:43	10:21	10:00	9:40	9:23	9:05	8:4
6	12:52	12:25	12:00	11:36	11:15	10:54	10:3
7	15:00	14:29	14:00	13:32	13:08	12:43	12:2
8	17:09	16:34	16:00	15:28	15:00	14:32	14:0
9	19:17	18:38	18:00	17:24	16:53	16:21	15:5
10	21:26	20:42	20:00	19:21	18:45	18:10	17:3
11	23:35	22:46	22:00	21:17	20:38	19:59	19:2
12	25:43	24:50	24:00	23:13	22:30	21:48	21:1
13	27:52	26:55	26:00	25:09	24:23	23:37	22:5
14	30:00	28:59	28:00	27:05	26:15	25:26	24:4
15	32:09	31:03	30:00	29:01	28:08	27:15	26:2
16	34:17	33:07	32:00	30:57	30:00	29:04	28:1
17	36:26	35:11	34:00	32:53	31:53	30:53	30:0
18	38:34	37:16	36:00	34:49	33:45	32:42	31:4
19	40:43	39:20	38:00	36:45	35:38	34:31	33:3
20	42:52	41:24	40:00	38:42	37:30	36:20	35:1
21	45:00	43:28	42:00	40:38	39:23	38:09	37:0
22	47:09	45:32	44:00	42:34	41:15	39:58	38:4
23	49:17	47:36	46:00	44:30	43:08	41:47	40:3
24	51:26	49:40	48:00	46:26	45:00	43:36	42:2
25	53:35	51:44	50:00	48:22	46:53	45:25	44:0
26	55:43	53:48	52:00	50:18	48:45	47:14	45:5
27	57:52	55:52	54:00	52:14	50:38	49:03	47:3
28	1:00:00	57:56	56:00	54:10	52:30	50:52	49:2
29	1:02:09	1:00:00	58:00	56:06	54:23	52:41	51:1
30	1:04:17	1:02:04	1:00:00	58:03	56:15	54:30	52:5
31	1:06:26	1:04:08	1:02:00	1:00:00	58:08	56:20	54:4
32	1:08:34	1:06:13	1:04:00	1:01:56	1:00:00	58:10	56:2
33	1:10:43	1:08:17	1:06:00	1:03:52	1:01:53	1:00:00	58:
34	1:12:52	1:10:21	1:08:00	1:05:48	1:03:45	1:01:49	1:00:0
35	1:17:09	1:12:25	1:10:00	1:07:44	1:05:38	1:03:38	1:01:4
36	1:19:17	1:14:29	1:12:00	1:09:40	1:07:30	1:05:27	1:03:3
37	1:21:26	1:16:34	1:14:00	1:11:36	1:09:23	1:07:16	1:05:
38	1:23:35	1:18:38	1:16:00	1:13:32	1:11:15	1:09:05	1:07:0
39	1:25:43	1:20:42	1:18:00	1:15:28	1:13:08	1:10:54	1:08:4
40	1:27:52	1:22:46	1:20:00	1:17:24	1:15:00	1:12:40	1:10:3
	28	29	30	31	32	33	34

miles per hour

35	36	37	38	39	40	miles
00:10	00:10	00:10	00:09	00:09	00:09	0.1
00:21	00:20	00:20	00:19	00:19	00:18	0.2
00:31	00:30	00:29	00:28	00:28	00:27	0.3
00:41	00:40	00:39	00:38	00:37	00:36	0.4
00:51	00:50	00:49	00:47	00:46	00:45	0.5
1:02	1:00	00:58	00:57	00:56	00:54	0.6
1:12	1:10	1:08	1:06	1:05	1:03	0.7
1:22	1:20	1:18	1:16	1:14	1:12	0.8
1:32	1:30	1:28	1:25	1:23	1:21	0.9
1:43	1:40	1:37	1:35	1:32	1:30	1.0
3:26	3:20	3:14	3:10	3:05	3:00	2
5:08	5:00	4:52	4:44	4:37	4:30	3
6:51	6:40	6:29	6:19	6:10	6:00	4
8:34	8:20	8:06	7:54	7:42	7:30	5
10:17	10:00	9:43	9:29	9:14	9:00	6
12:00	11:40	11:20	11:04	10:47	10:30	7
13:42	13:20	12:58	12:38	12:20	12:00	8
15:25	15:00	14:35	14:13	13:52	13:30	9
17:08	16:40	16:12	15:48	15:23	15:00	10
18:51	18:20	17:49	17:23	16:56	16:30	11
20:34	20:00	19:26	18:58	18:29	18:00	12
22:17	21:40	21:04	20:31	20:00	19:30	13
24:00	23:20	22:41	22:06	21:33	21:00	14
25:42	25:00	24:18	23:41	23:06	22:30	15
27:25	26:40	25:55	25:16	24:38	24:00	16
29:08	28:20	27:32	26:50	26:10	25:30	17
30:51	30:00	29:10	28:25	27:42	27:00	18
32:34	31:40	30:47	30:00	29:15	28:30	19
34:17	33:20	32:25	31:35	30:46	30:00	20
36:00	35:00	34:02	33:10	32:19	31:30	21
37:42	36:40	35:39	34:44	33:51	33:00	22
39:25	38:20	37:17	36:19	35:24	34:30	23
41:08	40:00	38:54	37:54	36:51	36:00	24
42:51	41:40	40:31	39:29	38:28	37:30	25
44:34	43:20	42:08	41:04	40:00	39:00	26
46:17	45:00	43:45	42:38	41:32	40:30	27
48:00	46:40	45:23	44:13	43:05	42:00	28
49:42	48:20	47:00	45:48	44:37	43:30	29
51:25	50:00	48:37	47:23	46:09	45:00	30
53:08	51:40	50:14	48:58	47:41	46:30	31
54:51	53:20	51:53	50:31	49:14	48:00	32
56:34	55:00	53:31	52:06	50:46	49:30	33
58:17	56:40	55:09	53:41	52:18	51:00	34
:00:00	58:20	56:46	55:16	53:50	52:30	35
:01:42	1:00:00	58:23	56:50	55:23	54:00	36
:03:25	1:01:40	1:00:00	58:25	56:55	55:30	37
:05:08	1:03:20	1:01:37	1:00:00	58:28	57:00	38
:06:51	1:05:00	1:03:14	1:01:35	1:00:00	58:30	39
:08:34	1:06:40	1:04:50	1:03:10	1:01:32	1:00:00	40
35	36	37	38	39	40	

be loaded with kid stuff. These are deadly serious competitions jammed with factory entries, since the car's ability, and the driver's skill are usually more closely defined in such big-time events. Quite often in a rally where snowy mountain passes are involved there will be an alternate route for those who are more "chicken" at heart—or sometimes, smarter.

In rallies like the Monte Carlo, more than half the field has been lost on a single leg, trying to cross a snowy Alp or an icy pass while still maintaining a good average speed. Men have been killed in these events, and many cars have been totally destroyed. Skilled rally drivers and navigators are quite often at a premium and have a choice of several cars to make the assault with. Because these trials usually involve a thousand or more miles and, at times, around-the-clock driving, they are a far cry from the family-fun-and-frolic junkets.

Before the event, the sharp rally man will appraise his chances of running into heavy snow and ice. For a summer event like the Alpine Rally, this is rarely a factor, except in the uppermost passes. If it is to be a winter snow run, he'll want a car with phenomenal traction and roadability. (This would automatically rule out most American cars.) In such a test, speed is not as important a factor as it is in the summer rally—for instance, the small, comparatively slow Renault Dauphine took the Monte Carlo Rally in 1958, because of its snowhandling capabilities.

A rear engine car has a traction advantage on snow, but, by the same token, may turn into a screaming nightmare while descending a slicked-ice Alp—a maneuver where front-engined cars are usually at their best. The famous Swedish Saab has won a number of rallies in snow and ice, and, on one notable occasion, two of these front-wheel-drive cars were the only cars to get over a bad icy pass—but they had to do it by backing up, which gave them more traction.

All major-event rally cars customarily carry various forms of de-ditching equipment which may include lightweight plow-type boat anchors with block-and-fall, at least two shovels, chains, bags of sand, picks, and some carry traction mats. In extreme cases, a length of ¼-inch nylon rope can be used as an added brake by wrapping it around a tree when descending a steep ice slope. Several wheel blocks, usually with nails driven through them, will help hold the car while the rope is moved forward to another tree or rock. This is serious stuff, and should only be attempted by top men in top cars.

Despite the hazards, quite often at the finish there will be a several-car tie. To break this tie, horrifying trials are often introduced. Once at Monte Carlo there were nearly a dozen cars who had finished the run with no loss of points. They were immediately shoved into a compound and no one was allowed to touch them or raise their hoods. Due to the high speeds and tough Alpine roads, the brakes on many of the finishing cars were in dreadful shape, some almost gone on all wheels, and, worse yet, some were without brakes on two alternate wheels.

Despite this, the next day the cars were brought to a starting line, facing a level straightaway about a mile long. Half way down this straightaway, though the distance was not exactly known, a white line was painted across the roadway. The cars were given just so many seconds to get to the other end, which called for extreme high speed.

The gimmick was that on the way to the other end, when crossing the white line, the cars had to come to a stop, back up completely over the white line and, then go ahead again. The brakes, now cold and untried by the drivers since the day before, couldn't be relied on. There was no warm-up. The cars were pushed to the line. Thirty seconds before the start (the cars ran one at a time), the steward signaled the driver to fire up his engine. After this brief warm-up, the flag was dropped and off he went.

When some of the cars reached the white line in the center of the course, they were doing close to 100 mph; jammed brakes caused them to spin, and in one case, the driver almost reached the finish before he could get his car stopped and into reverse. The event was won by a slower car that applied brakes just before reaching the line, slid over, backed up, and was then on its way again.

In other years, ties at Monte Carlo have been broken by timed high-speed runs from Monte Carlo up to the Grand Corniche Drive, which twists like a coiled snake and ends up in Nice. In addition, in these tie-breakers there are usually several detours employed, taking the cars off the Grand Corniche, down to the little Corniche below, then up a mountainous slope again, only to double back through the twisting streets of Monte Carlo itself to the finish. On these run-offs the navigator must be as sharp as a hoodlum's icepick, and the driver must be as alert as a benzedrine-addicted cat.

In the big-time events it is important for the factories to win, because the European buyer, being more cautious than his American counterpart, usually buys only on a put-up-or-shut-up basis. He knows that any car that has won a major rally must be a capable road car, and should serve him well under all conditions. In Europe, the technique of the Madison Avenue Ad Kid who verbally blows fiery breath into a real turkey to con millions of Americans out of their dollars wouldn't get off the ground. Our typical Ad Kid would be laughed into delirium tremens after his first foul-ball attempt at misinformation.

Gymkhanas

Another type of event usually requiring a driver—navigator team is the Gymkhana. Gymkhanas differ from rallies in that they are usually fun-driving events which may involve puncturing balloons with a pointed stick or parking between two closely-placed hay bales without touching them, or even driving blindfolded around a small course while the navigator instructs the driver to bear right, stop, or go ahead. Gymkhanas are often made-up, on-the-spot games for automobiles, and the whole event is usually played by ear, depending on the size of the group and the sobriety of same.

For the benefit of those who have never taken part in a rally, or for anyone who would like to organize a rally in his area, our good neighbors, the Lower Bucks County Sports Car Club, have loaned us the release and instruction sheet used in their "June Jump" Rally in 1958.

RELEASE

I hereby agree to hold harmless and keep indemnified the Lower Bucks County Sports Car Club, and their respective officials, representatives and agents from and against all actions, claims, costs, expenses and demands in respect of death, injury, loss or damage, to the person or property of myself, or of my passenger (s) or any spectator or other person, howsoever caused or arising out of or in connection with my entry or my taking part in this meeting, and notwithstanding that the same may have been contributed to or occasioned by the negligence of the said bodies, their officials, representatives or agents. I declare that while taking part in this rally or activity I have an operative policy of *liability insurance.*

Driver's Name ______________________________

Address ______________________________

Telephone No. ______________________________

Navigator's Name ______________________________

Address ______________________________

Telephone No. ______________________________

Make of Car __________ Model __________ Year __________

Signed ______________________________
Driver

Mileage ____________________

"JUNE JUMP" RALLY
LOWER BUCKS COUNTY SPORTS CAR CLUB

All clues can be seen from your car if you have very good vision or binoculars. Clues will be found on telephone poles, signs, bridges, mail boxes, etc.
Scoring will be computed on total mileage and elapsed time between Check Points. Each leg of this rally is independent of the other legs in relation to elapsed time, so do not give up if you feel you have done badly on one leg!

SCORING SYSTEM

6 points per minute early—2 points per minute late
4 points per mile under—2 points per mile over

YOU MAY BE DISQUALIFIED FOR THE FOLLOWING REASONS:

1. Stopping in sight of Check Point.
2. Violation of traffic regulations.
3. Missing a Check Point or not passing through them in proper order.
4. Drinking of intoxicating beverages during Rally competition.
5. Loss of time sheet.

Dirt roads *ARE* used in this Rally—they are marked as such on the Clue Sheet.
You will be permitted to take a pit stop at any Check Point.
A speedometer error of plus 5% will be allowed in your favor.
A ten (10) mile marker will show official Rally mileage.
Check Points will be maintained for thirty (30) minutes after last car is due.

GOOD LUCK! SEE YOU LATER!

HERE ARE YOUR CLUES—HAVE FUN FINDING THEM

1. L—First Possible—(Average Speed 25.9 MPH) Dirt
2. L—After The Shimps—Name on mailbox
3. R—Nemoral St. Dirt
   31

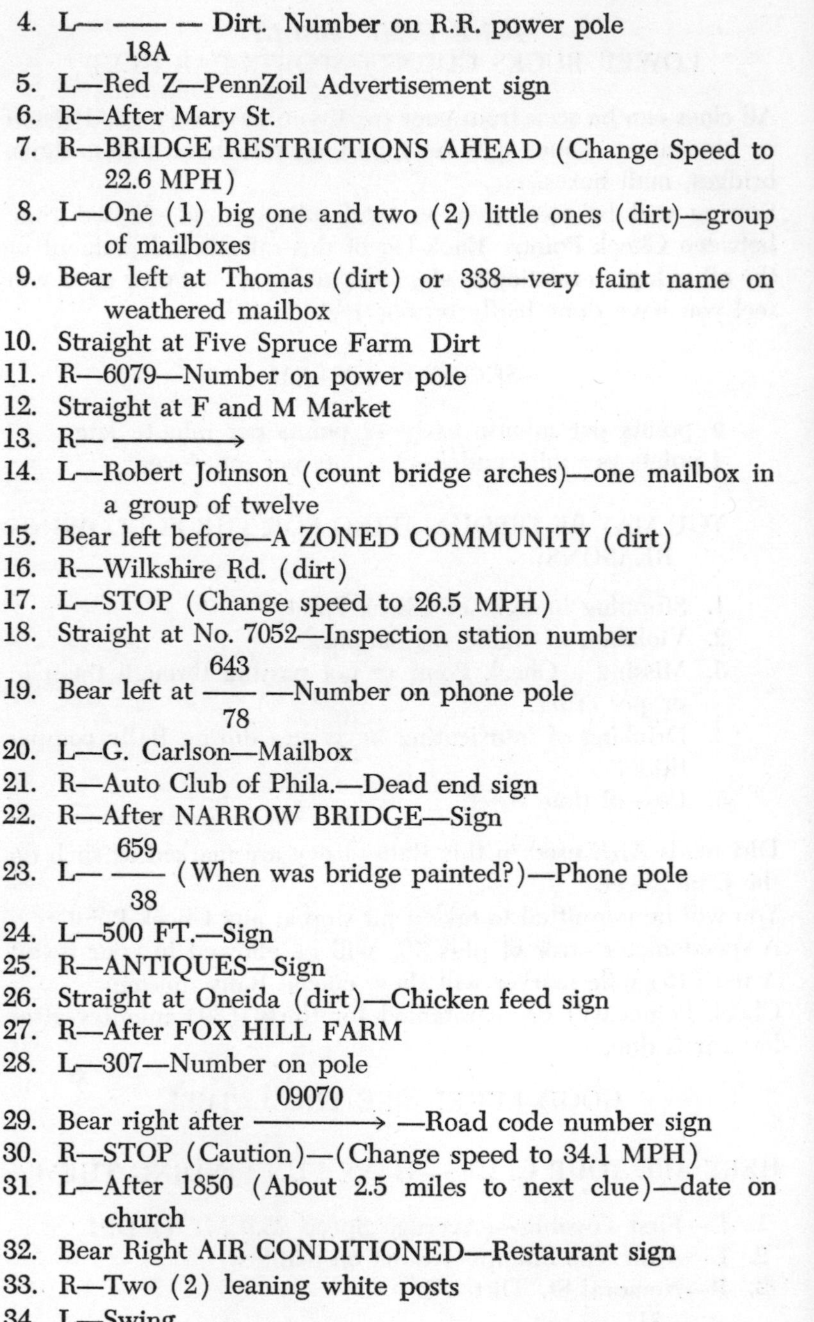

4. L— ——— — Dirt. Number on R.R. power pole
   18A
5. L—Red Z—PennZoil Advertisement sign
6. R—After Mary St.
7. R—BRIDGE RESTRICTIONS AHEAD (Change Speed to 22.6 MPH)
8. L—One (1) big one and two (2) little ones (dirt)—group of mailboxes
9. Bear left at Thomas (dirt) or 338—very faint name on weathered mailbox
10. Straight at Five Spruce Farm Dirt
11. R—6079—Number on power pole
12. Straight at F and M Market
13. R— ———→
14. L—Robert Johnson (count bridge arches)—one mailbox in a group of twelve
15. Bear left before—A ZONED COMMUNITY (dirt)
16. R—Wilkshire Rd. (dirt)
17. L—STOP (Change speed to 26.5 MPH)
18. Straight at No. 7052—Inspection station number
19. Bear left at $\frac{643}{78}$—Number on phone pole
20. L—G. Carlson—Mailbox
21. R—Auto Club of Phila.—Dead end sign
22. R—After NARROW BRIDGE—Sign
23. L—$\frac{659}{38}$ (When was bridge painted?)—Phone pole
24. L—500 FT.—Sign
25. R—ANTIQUES—Sign
26. Straight at Oneida (dirt)—Chicken feed sign
27. R—After FOX HILL FARM
28. L—307—Number on pole
29. Bear right after $\xrightarrow{09070}$ —Road code number sign
30. R—STOP (Caution)—(Change speed to 34.1 MPH)
31. L—After 1850 (About 2.5 miles to next clue)—date on church
32. Bear Right AIR CONDITIONED—Restaurant sign
33. R—Two (2) leaning white posts
34. L—Swing

35. Stay on Macadam
36. L—STOP (Count reflectors on stop sign)
37. Straight at LEHIGH CEMENT—Sign on supply store
38. Cross 563—Route number 563
39. Straight at Black Bell (dirt)—(Change speed to 17.1 MPH) —Iron bell in yard
40. Go towards 90961 (dirt)—Road code number sign
41. Straight at "Don't be a Game" (Start yourselves after 20 minute—Sign lunch break—Av. Speed 25.6 MPH)
42. Straight at SCHOOL BUS STOP
43. R— $\frac{\quad}{99}$ —Number on pole
44. L—R.F.D. 3—Mailbox
45. R—Sunburst stone (dirt)—Huge stone painted 4 different colors
46. L—Trout (Change speed to 22.1 MPH)—Sign with name and figure of Trout
47. Straight at $\frac{1}{59 \pm 32}$ —Number on pole
48. Stay on dirt
49. Bear left at Stop sign with bullet hole
50. L—Roman Catholic Church—Sign
51. R—After Parochial School (Change speed to 33.1 MPH)
52. L—Roman Catholic Church and follow route (6 mi. to next clue)—Sign
53. R—Before Esso—Gas station
54. Straight at STOP
55. Go toward Arthur Kichline (Change speed to 33.8 MPH)—Mailbox
56. R—7 Easton
57. Bear right at Stout's $\xrightarrow[\text{CENTER}]{\text{CIVIC}}$ —Sign
58. L—Volent—Sign
59. L—After Third Bridge
60. Straight at STOP
61. R— $\frac{8}{44 \pm 50}$ Road code number sign
62. Bear right at THE BABBLING BROOK (3.5 mi. to next clue)—Beer Joint

63. L—Seal Fast (Change speed to 23.3 MPH)—Tire patch ad.
64. Straight—State Game Lands—Sign
65. R—John F. Little—Sign
66. L—Permit #56—Very small print on back of Stop Sign
67. Bear right—Rock Ridge Chapel—Sign
68. L—09098—Road code number sign
69. R— $\frac{2}{60}$ (dirt)—Phone pole number
70. R—John Moodie (dirt)—Mailbox
71. L—Dead End and stay on macadam
72. L— 0 ± 00 —Road code number sign
73. Bear left at STOP—(About 1.5 mi. to next clue)
74. Bear left—Shore Route
75. Pick up 413 South and follow route (About 5½ mi. to next clue)
76. R—3 Doylestown
77. L—09132 (dirt)—Road code number sign
78. Straight at Colonial (dirt)—Sign—dealer in Antiques
79. R—Burlington Bristol Bridge
80. L—Antiques and stay on Furlong Road—Sign
81. Bear right at Stop sign
82. L—First possible
83. R— $\frac{1}{77 \# 75}$ —Road code number sign
84. L—09048—Road code number sign
85. R—Pruszenski (Caution) (dirt)—(Change speed to 20.8 MPH)—Mailbox
86. R—No Outlet (dirt)
87. L—340 (dirt)—Number on pole
88. L—Mill Rd. & York
89. L—Abbotts—Ice cream sign
90. R—After one lane bridge
91. Straight at STOP
92. R—Service—Garage
93. L—Signals Ahead

* FINIS *

Here is a sample of the blank slip used at every rally checkpoint to record the progress of each entry:

LEG #3

Car #

Time Out:

Time In:

Minutes Early: Points:

Minutes Late: Points:

Average Speed—29.3 MPH

And finally here are the sealed instructions participants opened at the end of the "June Jump" Rally:

SORRY,

DINNER WILL BE SERVED AT THE HATBORO MANOR
OLD YORK RDS. AND MONUMENT AVE.
HATBORO, PA.

6; 30

13

What To Do 'Til The Doctor Comes

YOUR SPORTS OR RALLY CAR, LIKE ANY AUTOMOBILE, may someday go *Poof!* sixty miles from Phoenix. It may die like a lovesick maiden just six miles from your dealer (and his questionable service), or it is quite possible that it may toss a rod in the middle of Texas. For such an occasion, the writer, having been in the sports car repair business, has one or two suggestions to make.

Nine times out of ten, when your sports car engine goes *Clunk!* and stops, the breakdown was caused by something so childish and insignificant that even a ten-year-old boy could effectively make the repair.

Finding the Trouble

Regardless of how the "purists" may beat their breasts, a lot of American car accessories are far superior to any made elsewhere in the world. English wiring particularly, and their electric fuel pumps, are much more susceptible to failure through dampness than our own. On these shores we have become used to slamming through deep puddles and running through snow (puddles that would drown out many top English cars in the first splash). It seems odd that in England, where it rains more often than it doesn't, they should build electrical systems (and, I might add, canvas tops) far less capable of coping with dampness than an American Ford or Chevrolet convertible. The points on electric fuel pumps often refuse to function if someone spills a glass of water within ten feet of them. The point I'm getting at, though, is that nine out of ten failures can quickly be remedied once you know what caused them.

There are two ways to approach an engine or car failure, or perhaps I should say three. One way (and sometimes the most sensible) is to put a torch to the car and collect on the insurance. There are some very neat ways of doing this, but it's quite a serious offense if you get caught.

For example, I once sold an expensive sports car of my own to a man who drove it to Richmond, Virginia, before deciding he didn't like it. Since the car was heavily insured against fire, he drove it out into the country from Richmond and deliberately set it afire. Unfortunately (for him), an unobserved farmer saw the whole operation, and my good customer became the stripe-suited guest of the state for some time. So if you must set your car on fire for the insurance keep a sharp lookout to make sure you are not being watched.

The second (and best) way to approach a car failure on the highway, before even getting out from behind the wheel, is to leisurely stretch yourself and perhaps mutter, "Well, I'll be a three-headed Laplander!"

After this, light up a cigarette or pipe. Then, if you insist, *casually* lift the hood. Observe all the wiring as if you couldn't be less interested, because something like a coil wire might have jumped out of place. It is also a good idea to check the fuel supply.

If you have a slight knowledge, or even an expert knowledge of engines, it is most important that you get yourself in the right frame of mind for solving the problem *before* you tackle it. Try to approach the failure like a disinterested kibitzer and your chances of success will be much better. Regardless of how urgent it is that you reach the next town quickly, don't allow yourself to become panicked. You may be in the middle of the Alcan highway, just twenty wheel-turns ahead of a raging blizzard which will bury you in a few short hours, but I still say, take it easy.

The panicky (or third) way to approach a stalled car is to start pulling things out, twisting adjustments, and wearing your battery down to counter-check each twist to see if it worked—until the car is hopelessly out of tune and couldn't possibly run even if it had gas (which it didn't).

If you have a knowledge of automobile engines, lazily test for spark at the plugs, then for gas at the carburetor. If you have both of these, and didn't hear any expensive noises as you stopped, get behind the wheel, turn the key and start her up—she's *got* to go.

If you don't have fuel at the carburetor but have it in the tank, the chances are the fuel filter is clogged or the points in the electric pump aren't functioning. You may even have a loose wire at the pump. Anyway, remove the cover shielding the pump points and run a nail file or piece of paper between the points. This will usually get it going again.

If you haven't any spark at the plugs, check for spark at the coil. If there's none there, check the distributor points. Through lack of adjustment or care the fiber

The dean of all sports car drivers, 70-year-old John L. Rutherfurd, and his D-Jaguar, after doing 164 mph at Daytona Beach.

(Photo by Daniel R. Rubin)

Phil Hill, probably the greatest American race driver today, in his winning Ferrari during the 1957 Nassau Speed Week.

John Fitch, manager of the Lime Rock track and the only American ever to become a member of the Mercedes factory team.

"Gentleman Jim" Kimberly, of Kleenex fame, entertains the gallery with a practice pit stop at Sebring.

Fallen Lotus, dewheeled, rests at sideline.

Most of these citizens will stand here for the entire 24 Hours of LeMans.

Ricardo Rodriguez, the youngest driver ever to hit the big time, with his sister before a race start. Rodriguez was 15 when he began winning major events, though, because of his age, he has not yet been allowed to compete in the States.

More fortunate citizens enjoy the June endurance classic at the bar.

(Photo by Daniel R. Rubin)

Camera-bug wears coveralls to snap Jag's progress in British-type hillclimb, combining some stickier features of a field trial, run off at Skytop, Pennsylvania.

(Photo by Daniel R. Rubin) *Do they call this a road?*

Vintage Bugatti leads Concours d'Elégance through Watkins Glen, New York. (Photo by Daniel R. Rubin)

Two MG's and a Jag pulled over at checkpoint in Devil's Delight Rally held near Westchester (New York) Airport by MG Car Club. (Photo by Daniel R. Rubin)

One of the greatest of all rally cars, the Volvo, being bent hard around a corner on a dirt road in New Jersey.

Shades of Cervantes, with ballons for windmills and a brand-new Alfa to replace Rosinante, in this Westchester County gymkhana.

(Photo by Daniel R. R

With fastidious aplomb, a British team at LeMans shows the correct way to operate on a sports car.

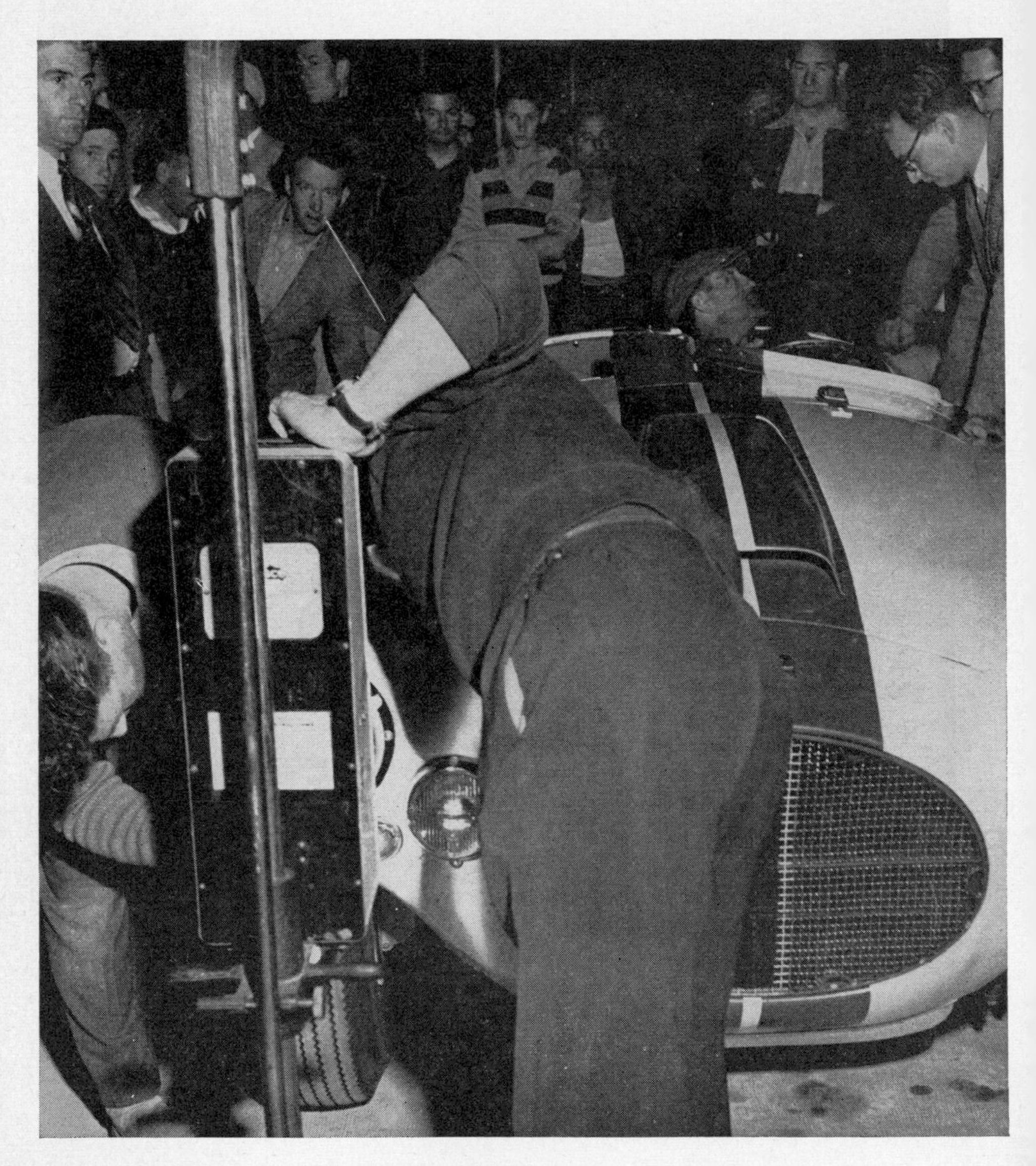

No place for inexactitude . . . an entry gets its headlights adjusted to LeMans specifications.

To the devoted race technician, a car is never ready, and spark plugs are changed right up to the starting gun. This adjustment, however, is quite legal.

If they ever come through just right, half the fun will be gone, as attested by these two additional Jag pictures.

rubbing block may have worn down enough so that the points no longer open.

Basket Cases

Most of the time these elementary checks will reveal the source of the trouble. More expensive breakdowns, like a collapsed piston or a ruptured doohickey, call for thorough knowledge, correct tools, and replacement parts to overcome trouble before you can start off again. If you are handy with tools and your sports car calls for weird sizes (either English, Whitworth, or Metric), it's not a bad idea to carry a selective set of these with you at all times. If you should have a breakdown in East Adam's Apple, Arkansas, that the local Cadillac man could fix (or replace the part when it's air-mailed in), unless he has the right tools he'll be as stumped as ever. The Snap-On Tool Company in America makes excellent wrenches and sockets for all foreign cars.

A minimum kit of these tools might be a wise thing to keep with you on long junkets, always. It is also a wise precaution, when traveling long distances with a sports car, to have a complete, nation-wide list of foreign car service stations with you at all times. These are available at most dealers. It is surprising today how many small, out-of-the-way towns now have full-fledged sports car dealerships and service facilities. In fact, it is almost impossible today to drive anywhere in the U.S. and be more than a few hours away from competent foreign car service.

Regardless of how minor or major your sports car trouble may be, that calm attitude and casual appraisal on your part will pay off in big dividends, even if you happen to be the service manager for the Ferrari race team.

Tune-up

Engine tune-up is where most sports cars in competition come apart at the seams. These untidily groomed steeds are often the victims of incompetent know-it-alls, so lacking for engine feel that they couldn't tune a one-string ukulele in thirty years.

This writer has come to one basic conclusion, and that is that in addition to mechanical knowledge a real tune-up man must have a tenth-sense feel for the engine itself. Show me the mechanic who pops out his chest and announces, "I don't need any fancy gadgets to tune a car, all I need to do is listen to the engine." Show me this man and I will show you an over-egotistical *dope*. Such a man doesn't live and never did live.

True, there are many cases in which a good man *can* make an adjustment or diagnose a fault by ear, but there are many more cases where he *can't*—so beware of a guy with a screwdriver and a dirty rag who approaches the most complicated engines as if they were Tinker-Toy sets.

The good tune-up man thinks like an engine. He can actually feel in his veins the timing that is off, or a valve that's set up too hard. He really has a "feel" and with this comes respect.

When making final adjustments he's not too proud to use instruments to double-check himself. You will often find that on the simplest jobs, such as adjusting ignition points, he takes four times as long as Hurricane Hooligan, who whips through these menial tasks in a flash. The difference is that the boy taking the longer time checks and double-checks every operation, and won't pass it until he's thoroughly assured himself that the adjustment is perfect.

The reason we have so many lousy mechanics and

tune-up men can, I believe, be traced directly to Detroit's flat-rate service system that puts a premium on speed. In cases I actually know about, thorough experts have been fired because they were too slow.

For example, let's consider an unnamed company dealer service that charges $3.00 for a tune-up on its Humpty-Dumpty 6½. This brush tune-up calls for a quick glance at the plugs, a check of the distributor points, and an adjustment of the idling screws on the carburetor—period. It is possible, under this ridiculous system, for Flashy Oscar to whip through as many as five tune-ups in an hour. This means big money for the shop as they get, on the average, 60 per cent of the labor, plus any parts involved.

Theoretically, the $3.00 tune-up charge under the flat-rate system was to pay for a mechanic to spend slightly over an hour on the unfortunate owner's car. As it quite often works out, the tune-up man racks up four or five hours' pay for himself and the shop out of every single hour. Tune-up instruments cost money, service space costs money—so, for this reason, a real good tune-up man who might actually spend an hour or more on an engine will be losing money for the shop as well as for himself; he'd stand an excellent chance of getting fired. Bear in mind good men like this *have* been fired just for giving the customer what he paid for.

As sad a commentary as it is, quality workmanship is no longer considered a premium by many shops. In my thirty years of working on automobiles and visiting service shops from coast to coast and across the ocean, I have never met a single dozen men I would rate as expert tune-up men. In the past, I have worked in huge shops with dozens of expert mechanics who could overhaul and build engines to perfection—but then couldn't make them go right because they didn't have the "feel" a good tune-up man must have. Men like the late Clay Smith, who serviced the Lincolns that won the Mexican Road Race and many other top race cars, just can't be found in every city or even in every state.

Because sports cars are usually much more sensitive to correct adjustments, a good tune-up man is more essential in this field than in the field of the family sedan. I have met, however, men who were experts on getting the last rpm out of a Jaguar or MG who fell flat on their faces when tackling a Ferrari or Osca.

If you ever intend to run cars in competition of any type, your most essential equipment will be a good tune-up man. Even if he charges you double rates, it's still cheap.

Another type of mechanic to beware of is the sleazy character who can fix anything from a transmission or front end to the engine and brakes. There is only one thing I am 100 per cent positive about in this life, and that is, there is no such thing in the entire world as a good *all-around* mechanic.

For a man to become a perfectionist in engine work and tune-up, he must invest between ten and fifteen years of his life. A good front end man must also spend years at work and study; so must a transmission, brake, or any other unit man. The simple fact is, a human being doesn't live long enough to become a real perfectionist in every field pertaining to the automobile.

A good man who works on just carburetors and ignition can spend the better part of ten years just learning how to get the most out of each of these two items. If he is to be *really* good on several types of sports car carburetors and ignition systems, he won't be able to do it in ten years. A good carburetor man has rebuilt hundreds of carburetors from the ground up. A good carburetor builder alone must have six years behind him.

For this reason, when a handsome, smiling mechanic with six months of G.I. training behind him announces, "Bring your Ferrari in, Doc, whatever's wrong, we'll find it and fix it, 100 per cent," slip the Ferrari in gear and head for the next shop.

Naturally, every sports car dealer claims he has a *whiz,* always ready and willing to service your newly-acquired gem. The cold facts in the matter are that, in two of New York's largest sports car shops, *real* mechanics are as rare as polar bears in the Mojave Desert. It so happens in these two cases that the owners of the dealerships are so ignorant of mechanical know-how themselves they'd have a hard time differentiating between a bootblack and a grease-monkey.

14

Cheating for Fun and Profit

IN THE REALM OF SPORTS CARS, AND OTHER COMPETITION cars that have been designed for general use, there are usually methods for hopping them up for better performance. Production sports cars and competition cars, including rally and stock cars, usually have an endurance factor built into them that will not be found in the out-and-out racing sports car.

Cars of the touring (rally) class must have endurance, because many of these will be purchased by buyers with no intention of racing them, but purely for the pleasure derived from owning such cars. For this reason, by "endurance" we mean that these cars should be able to travel thousands of miles without a breakdown or important overhaul. On the other hand, the racing sports car that is trailed to and from race courses may be completely rebuilt, engine-wise, after each hard run of 100 miles. At the least, rings and valves may require replacement. Many components of racing car engines are built thinner and lighter than the corresponding parts of cars designed for endurance. Thus they can't be expected to wear as long.

Now, we know that you wouldn't think of cheating, but we're inserting this chapter sort of as a public service in case you are mildly interested or know of a friend who might like to become a thief and cop a lot of "production" class silverware. In the first place, it's quite possible to do considerable hopping up to most production engines without impairing their longevity by more than a percentage point or two. Hopped-up machines have gone through an entire race season without an important failure because in many cases the manufacturer built in safety factors beyond the needed point of endurance.

In production car racing, inspection is quite often tacky, to say the least (especially in sports cars) and only becomes tough in major competitions. Even then, many tricks have passed right under an inspector's eagle eye without ruffling one little feather. Good race engine setup men know most of the pitfalls of inspection, and try to design around them. In the average weekend, or small sports car contest, and even in some of the larger events, the inspector is quite often just a motoring rustic with a working knowledge of combustion theory. Some of these characters I've observed at sports car events would consider themselves quite sharp if they caught a guy carrying an entire extra cylinder assembly. Personally, I've had teams of inspectors working for me at the Daytona Beach Speed Trials who have been dealing with thieves for years, and therefore know most of the tricks, but even they get caught off base once in a while.

For example, several years ago we had a sports car running in the speed trials that was a lot faster than it should have been. We ripped this rig apart down to the last cotter key and never found a single trace of how the owner-driver had jiggled the grinder. ("Jiggled" is the standard term for altering production engines illegally.) This guy had jiggled, and though I had a team of five top inspectors checking, to this day I'm still wondering how he did it. We've caught many, but the cleverest cheating quite often came from factory teams where it was possible for the factory to supply an off-size part with the right-type part number. The only way we could disqualify the entry was by checking against published specifications.

Although cheating, conniving and general well-rounded dishonesty are actions universally frowned upon in the world of sport, since the birth of automobile racing more than a half century ago illegal hop-ups have been practiced by a variety of technicians. Lightening flywheels for whippier acceleration, reboring and installing larger pistons for greater displacement, are almost standardized methods, and universal speed-shop tricks. This chapter will not be concerned with common-place hop-ups, but will go deeper into jiggling that can't be detected by anyone not fully versed in the art of alteration thievery. Since the writer has searched out many such crooks in the line of duty, let me assure the sceptic that some of the boys I've bucked against were fantastically cunning at the gentle art of deception. These men can put from 10 to 20 mph on almost any car built today, and do it in such a way that even the manufacturer wouldn't have a clue.

Good inspectors have a feeling for these race technicians similar to the odd admiration top detectives have for Willie (The Actor) Sutton or the guys who pulled the Brink's job. It's a matching of wits, but as one hop-up genius told me when he got caught with an engine he claimed he "jiggled just a bit," "It's getting so it hardly pays to do good work anymore." Going to the other side of the fence for this chapter, I cornered several expert jigglers and asked them to level with me, which they did. One well-known conjurer told me that he'd gladly spill everything except the one trick he hadn't been caught at yet.

Honor Among Thieves

I believe I should state, at the outset, that many top mechanics have a code of honor which they maintain among themselves. For example, most of the real good ones would just as soon betray their country as work foreign equipment into their cars, like specially made non-stock cams or special racing pistons. As one said to me, "That would be outright cheating." They take their pride, and rightly so, in making a bomb out of an automobile by using only the stock parts, including the camshaft that came with the car. True, they may use optional parts made by the manufacturer for the car, but every part they use is a factory stock part, re-worked. If some wiseguy in their midst breaks this code, his fellow conspirators, if they find out, will turn him over to the inspectors in an eyeblink. On the other hand, they may know how Joe Blow has hopped his car legitimately—by their code—and they'd never open their mouths, though it might cost them several big races. To many of them it is a game to be played squarely against the inspectors, and that's the way they operate.

Balancing

The most important single item in setting up a production engine for racing is to have everything balanced to zero tolerance. This is where the factory jobs fall apart. Every valve, every piston, in fact every moving part from the crankshaft to the water pump must be balanced. Take cylinder heads. When the average yo-yo takes a compression reading of your engine and finds that you have, for example, 140 pounds of compression in the first cylinder, 125 in the next, perhaps 120 in the next, and maybe 132 in the last, the typical explanation is, you need a valve job, ring job, or even a new head gasket.

Nine times out of ten your local serviceman will tell you that you're losing compression by the rings or valves, and seven times out of ten he's wrong. As top race men know, the head has probably domed, i.e., warped, so that it now forms an arch. The center of the head is actually domed from the ends because of unequal dissipation of heat, since the center cylinders usually run hotter. To check this, the race mechanic uses a c.c. (cubic centimeter) glass to get the *exact* capacity of each cylinder. In the case of a domed head, which is more common than not, he will remove it and grind the ends of the head down until he has a perfectly balanced capacity in all cylinders. Some strict inspectors might spot this end grinding and disqualify the car for having shaved heads —in spite of the fact that it is a master stroke of tune-up. To beat the inspector hazard in a big race, the mechanic quite often will install brand-new heads, even though they will most likely be domed, too, before the race is over.

Smoothing

The hard thing for an inspector to spot because of carbon deposits, is the fact that the good race man has removed all sharp edges around the pistons, the heads, and even the spark plug holes. Sharp edges attract carbon, which becomes white-hot and may burn a hole through the piston. On the inside of the spark plug holes the race man rounds the edges, and on pistons with designs or names on the top, he will grind them off, since they are favored spots for damaging carbon to collect.

Valving

The next most important part of hop-up work pertains to the camshaft and valving. The big thing with valves is to keep them from floating at high rpms, and there are several ways this is done. "Floating" means that the valve action is so fast that the valves never fully shut, and this naturally dissipates much of the compression and charge force of the cylinder. The valve springs for a race car must be stronger than stock if the car is to hit its maximum top speed. It's usually illegal to change valve springs, but there are methods of improving the performance of stock equipment. The common way is to shim the springs with washers from the bottom so that the spring is actually shortened, and the tension increased. Some of the smarter operators make complete valves, cutting the valve spring keeper lower down to compress the spring further. Another way is to cut an additional case lock for the keeper in a standard valve, 1/16″ to 1/8″ below the original cut, and pray that a good inspector won't see that the valve has two grooves.

Another valve trick, which can only be discovered on complete disassembling, is lightened valves. The lighter the valve, the tighter the engine can turn up before float sets in. Most production valves are much too heavy for maximum horsepower, since they are built with an endurance factor in mind. However, to increase power and speed some engine life must be sacrificed, so the valves are lightened. In races where the inspection might be a bit sloppy, the valves are cut from the top side, but where inspection is apt to be rough, metal is ground away from the bottom. The race men remove as much from the valve as they possibly can without making it weak. The amount that you can remove from a valve without having any breakdown trouble would toss some engineers into a tailspin. For example, if the valve head is ¼″ thick in the center where it joins the stem, this can be reduced by half without any bad effects. This single action can easily add 300 rpms to a production engine.

On intake valves, where the engines are built with 45 degree seats, top men have found that they will be much better off with 30 or even 25 degree seats. The exhausts are usually held to 30 to avoid burning. This is a delicate operation, because reducing the valve seat angle also reduces the heat dissipation area of the valve. To get around this the race boys, knowing that the production seats are right in the middle, move the valve seats to the very outside edge on both the intake and exhaust, or, as the term goes, they "hang it right on the edge." The intake valve seat should not be wider than 1/16″ and 15/1000″ wider on the exhaust. The wider the valve is made through cutting, the further out the seat must be moved toward the edge; and the narrower these seats are made, the more horsepower. The reason for this is that you are actually increasing the working diameter of the valves.

Rocker Arms

Rocker arms are another spot that gets the race man's undivided attention. In some cases where the race man is afraid of jiggling the lifter or cutting the pushrods, the rocker arm is altered to increase the lift of the cam. This was done for many years by welding the natural hole in the rocker arm shut and drilling a new hole to increase the ratio from the pushrod to the valve, and thus giving the same effect as a high-lift cam.

Camshafts

Reworking stock camshafts is not too hard, and here's how it's done. Nearly all production camshafts are set for maximum economy and smooth running, and it's the race man's job to move them around to the point where you get the most horsepower, which is usually someplace where the manufacturer hasn't got it. The most important part in setting a camshaft is to find the crossover point. That's the spot where the lift is exactly the same on the intake valve opening and the exhaust valve closing, and the most important point of any camshaft. If you set it right you can practically get as much out of it as you can get out of an out-and-out racing cam. When you know your crossover, the cam can be advanced or retarded in many ways, such as by relocating the gear key or, if it's a bolt-on gear, relocating the hole, or by moving the gear on the crankshaft. This gear-moving can sometimes be pretty hard for an inspector to spot, even though he knows the car is running like a race engine.

Carburetion

There are a few tricks that can be done with fuel and carburetion, but it's hard to do anything that can't be detected. In some cars, all that is needed to increase power by as much as 10 or 15 horses is to raise the float level and increase the size of the fuel line. Most gas lines are much too small for high-performance running, and the fittings from the fuel tank to the fuel pump and into the carburetor should all be drilled out for a faster gas flow. Though this is illegal in many cases, it'll make a car go a lot faster.

Mechanical fuel pumps are always worked over

when the race men can get away with it, since the stock pressure is much too low for speed. Increasing the relief valve pressure in the pump to 5 or 5½ pounds may mean the difference between winning or losing a race. One well-known make of stock fuel pump *can't* be stepped up, and many cars that use this make have failed for this reason alone.

In the carburetor itself, a common trick is to open the main discharge nozzles for races on tracks where a lot of acceleration is needed. For faster tracks, where constant high speed is maintained, stock carburetor jets are usually adequate. Most carburetors on American engines haven't enough breathing capacity, even on the four-barrel jobs. Stock car race men have found that with a 300-cubic-inch engine or bigger, a venturi size of 1⅟₁₆″ or larger for each barrel is needed, and many of these jobs have a venturi size of one inch, or even less. This starves the engine at high speed. Many a car has been disqualified for opening the venturis just the way the factory should have done it in the first place.

Ignition

Most of the race men I spoke to, and this'll be a surprise to a lot of readers, felt that they could not improve performance by adding hot coils or condensers, or by replacing the distributors. These parts, they feel, need the least changing, though there have been some tricks for increasing the point spring tension to avoid high-speed bounce.

Spark plugs are extremely important. Naturally, the right heat range for the race to be run must be considered and the plugs gapped in the neighborhood of .020. A common practice is to saw off the ground electrode of the plug so that it does not completely overlap the center electrode. The ground electrode is shortened so that its end is in line with the middle of the center electrode. This will give quicker burning and a better all-around explosion. After the electrode has been sawed, the sharp edges should be ground off to avoid a hot spot developing on the plug. This could turn it into a constant-glow plug, one of the quickest ways of blowing the top of a piston off. Shortening the electrode is a legal trick.

"Fuel"

The "fuel" users, ("fuel" in the race trade means various derivitives of nitro, including nitrous oxide or so-called "laughing gas,") are another group entirely. Most top race men stay away from using "fuel" because of the hazard of having the driver cinderized in the event of a crash, or just an ordinary explosion from the heat. Some "fuel" users use milder concoctions which only add 15 or 20 mph to the car, providing the engine holds together. The newest and simplest way of applying "fuel" during a race or speed trial is to put the gook in the car's windshield washer container and reverse the hoses, so that when a button is pushed a charge of crash-dash shoots right into the intake manifold.

Other places where "fuels" have been stored have been in glove compartment tanks, under the instrument panel, in the doors, and in seat cushions. Another use for auxiliary tanks is to carry an extra fuel supply for long races where an extra pit stop for gas could easily cost the race. These are put in the same places as the nitro tanks, only they are usually much larger. A well-known race driver once got a slight skull fracture when his car flipped on a turn. What crushed his helmet was not the simple roll-over, but a gas tank hidden in the headlining that tore loose and conked him on the first bounce.

Pistons

One thing that had the good inspectors stopped for some time—and can still fool many—are reworked pistons, which used to be common throughout the race trade. The piston skirts were ground away from top to bottom so that the only parts of the piston that touched were the extreme top and bottom rings. This served two purposes. It cut the friction in half and lightened the entire piston assembly. All rings but the compression rings were filed out, and the compression edge was reduced to give the least possible contact while maintaining a seal. The cutaway pistons were given figure eight grooves to make oil reservoirs and even the cylinder walls were honed with a 100-grit stone in figure eights to hold the oil between the top and bottom of the piston; oil droplets ride up and down with the piston like an oil ball bearing.

Lubrication and Cooling

Water circulation can be slowed by trimming the impeller blades of the water pump. This accomplishes two things. It lessens the drag of the pump and allows the water to stay in the block just a fraction longer, letting it absorb just a bit more heat. Oil aerating in the crankcase sump is a major hazard since it allows air bubbles to enter the line. This at times, can cause a lubrication block similar to the vapor lock in a fuel line. Detergent oils are particular patsies for this. To overcome this possibility, some of the boys relocated the oil reservoir sump and pulled it out of the filter (which had the cartridge removed) or even out of the camshaft sump. Oil pressure can be increased by cutting the relief valve spring.

Transmissions

Some automatic transmissions can be reworked very simply. For example, take the big Chrysler transmission with its twelve quarts of oil. By draining ten of these quarts you have accomplished the same effect as shaving a flywheel, a very important move for fast acceleration. Removing ten quarts of oil from the Chrysler transmission will reduce the 0-60 time by almost 3 seconds, since the ten quarts of oil removed represent a considerable sum of spinning weight. On cars modified in this way, no noticeable damage was experienced in short races. However in longer races the boys carry seven or eight quarts, which still makes them considerably faster than if they carried the standard load.

Blocking off the heat riser to keep the temperature of the fuel down is an old trick that few hep drivers ever try any more. Another trick recently caught by the inspectors was a hand fuel pump which the driver operated through a hole in the front seat, just like the old race cars of 50 years ago. He had sealed the tank vent, and with this pump he could build up as much as 10 or 12 pounds fuel pressure, which kept him from starving in the corners, and he won quite a few races before this was discovered.

Many cars have tried to get by with ratchet-type rear ends to keep them from spinning in the corners, and one fellow got away with this for a long time. He was discovered when he broke a rear axle and the wheel came off, axle and all, while he continued under power to his pit more than half a mile away. Another race trick which means a few extra rpms is to charge the battery to the hilt before a race and then set the voltage regulator so that the generator won't operate at all. By doing this, all you have to turn is the weight of the armature.

Some more tricks that have been pulled include shaving the blocks instead of the heads to raise compression. As inspection got tougher, shaving the head was strictly for amateurs, and they got caught every time. For some time, however, the smarter boys got away with shaving the tops of the blocks, which accomplished the same thing.

One of the greatest jobs I ever ran across was pulled by a guy who had an irresistible Dale Carnegie personality and a magnificent set of tools. He was always offering his tools and help to the inspectors, especially his micrometers and steel rulers. It was a long time before the boys found out that this character had a complete set of measuring tools worth hundreds of dollars that had been custom-built for him to measure size his way. For example, if his engine was supposed to have a 4½" stroke, it did on his rule, but it would have a 4¾" stroke on anyone else's. For miking the heads, valves, or camshafts, he also had off-beat instruments. He's no longer allowed in the inspection compounds.

One trick that was caught this year for the first time was pulled by a driver who had tediously built up metal on his crankshaft so that when oversize bearings were fitted to the bottoms of the connecting rods, the metal, being on the bottom side of the crank, pulled the piston down a good ¼ inch further, giving the engine a longer stroke and a bigger firing charge. On American engines with hydraulic valve lifts, shortening of the pushrods has become the latest method of getting more rpms. With a shortened pushrod the oil-filled valve lift doesn't get pumped up all the way, and resists floating for as much as another 300 to 500 rpms. The amateurs who do this grind away the pushrod *ends,* which are case-hardened, to a point where they quickly wear away and reach total failure before the end of a short or medium-size race. The real pros cut the rod in two, take out what they want, and weld it together again, thus preserving the case-hardened ends, which will last forever.

There are dozens of methods for hopping up any engine, including Grand Prix engines, where it's legal. The purpose of this chapter was not to encourage the reader to stray from the sportsman's code, but to show his sister some of the things she might do for him, if she feels real bitchy.

15

Will Racing Be Outlawed?

In a country as large and vast as ours, it's only natural that the temperament and mentality of the population should run the full gamut from A to Z-cubed. Unfortunately, many Z-cubists have gotten into our legislatures. Due to some of the facets of our democratic government, politics have proved a haven for men who could succeed at nothing else. Some politicians are just dandy (as they might say at Cerutti's Bar) while others are frustrated hams; early-thwarted thespians who flunked high school dramatics but succeeded handsomely on the porkbarrel circuit. An unhealthy percentage of these have a flair for publicity that winds up with carefully thought-out off-beat statements. There seems to be a set formula to arouse the rabble. For example, if a senator or congressman should make the statement that "tan shoe polish is immoral and should be banned" there are enough fuzzy-heads in the guttery districts who will shout, "Hear, hear!" One of the best tools the publicity-minded politician has is the "safety pitch." Everyone wants to be safe. So all a guy has to do to get a group of moronic followers is to make statements like, "Back porches are unsafe" or, "Elm trees are dangerous to our very existence" and he'll get a bunch of wild-eyes to go along with him.

Now, the real wary politician, always striving for national attention, is too canny to weigh a campaign on one pitch such as safety alone; he adds a lot of irrelevant issues to tag onto safety's tail such as "demoralizing" ... "bloodthirsty" ... "wanton cxploitation." The fact that automobile racing of all types is an undeniable thrill sport, as well as a science, makes the sport a real juicy target for any evangelistic legislator to beat a tattoo on his bony chest over. For some years there have been congressional and senatorial noises about banning automobile competition of all types. Some have even gone so far as to compare auto racing with bullfighting and cockfighting, mass blood-letting, and Be Kind to Lions Week with Christian Bon-Bons in Rome. Some well-meaning safety organizations are also patsies for this sort of thinking and abhor auto racing, feeling that it encourages our younger warm-blooded sprouts to participate in daredevil tactics on the highway.

Despite all safety organization efforts to emasculate our mechanically-minded youth, a group of hairy-chested young men somehow survive the pantywaist dictums, and occasionally when they have an urge to see just what the old family bus will do on the turnpike, they follow that impulse and find out. For some of them it's the last thing they ever find out—but thousands get away with it every year. When writers like myself suggest legalized, policed drag strips on the local level where anyone with the urge can, for a small fee of a dollar or two, find out what Old Six-Cylinder Nell will do, the safety boys recoil like a dove of peace from a cobra: "Horrors, this encourages speeding." Hogwash. As anyone older than three knows, the automobile is a more dangerous weapon than a cannon, if properly aimed, and it has a potential killing power greater than that of a company of well-armed soldiers, under the right circumstances. Telling red-blooded Americans (or, for that matter, red-blooded citizens of any country), "No, No, don't touch!" is similar to telling girls to keep away from boys.

Years ago, I lived in an apartment house on the East River in New York. It was in the early days of the Depression and in the apartment next to me was a young fellow who'd just bought all the equipment for an African hunting trip when he ran out of money. He had to go to work in order to get up lunch money, but one item remained from the safari that never took place. This was an expensive elephant gun he'd bought at Abercrombie & Fitch, and a box of shells for it. We were neighbors for almost three years, and occasionally when I'd join him for a drink he'd get the gun out of a closet, dry-fire it a few times at imaginary charging beasts, and then return it to the closet, with what always seemed to be a touch of regret. He had never fired the gun once, but I knew he'd hung a lot of hopes on doing just that. Well, one hot July Sunday morning, just after daylight, a terrific blast and roar shattered the dawn stillness. I was out of bed in a flash and realized almost at once what had happened. I beat it out my door and pounded on his. He opened it, gun still in hand and whiter than a fresh bottle of milk. After three years of frustration he had finally shot the gun; right across the East River that bullet went, to rest somewhere in Brooklyn, I trust in Ebbett's Feld. As other doors started to open, I pushed him back in his room. I then asked the other neighbors, "Did you hear that explosion? What was it?" No one knew, and as far as I know to this day, no one ever found out. Later that morning, over coffee, he repeated several times, "Tom, I just *had* to do it. Hope it didn't hit someone." I listened to the news reports on the radio many times that day, and carefully searched the paper the following morning. Apparently the bullet, fully spent, had landed somewhere in the city where Murder, Inc., got its start, and had landed unnoticed.

A 300-plus horsepower automobile is not too unlike that elephant gun. Its owner, who may be as timid as Murphy's mouse and as conservative as a Chase Bank executive's funeral, will someday, somewhere, find the urge to shoot off his elephant gun almost irresistible, if he still has all the physical properties he was born with. My point (as it has been for years): "Give the man a place to shoot off his elephant gun and he won't do it on Main Street." In the past thirty years, I've known just about all the great competition drivers in the world. They've fired *their* elephant guns on the speedways; therefore, as a group, they are the most conservative, cautious and courteous drivers who travel the world's highways when they're just going from good old Point A to Point B, or down to the store. You'll never find the real pro burning up tires with jackrabbit starts on Main Street on Saturday night; and you'll never find one whipping through turnpike traffic at 80 mph when he should be doing 60 mph. In some sections of the country (which are more civilized than other parts) legalized drag strips are in operation today. In some other parts they've been frowned on and legally stomped out by bone-headed do-gooders. A case such as this happened recently near Philadelphia. To sum this thought up . . . "Who ever heard of rape in Paris?"

Automobile racing itself has done more to make this country safe for democracy than the last five Presidents of the United States. If you think this calls for a little explaining, here it is: The average person today, filled to the navel with TV commercials and exaggerated advertising in newspapers and magazines, probably thinks that a group of bright-eyed little engineers in Michigan, equipped with clip-boards, slide rules and white coats, are responsible for a big percentage of our automotive advances. By the same token, they probably feel that a group of dedicated flyboys and Pentagon Generals were responsible for our military vehicles and fighting planes that helped us beat the Nips and Krauts in World War Two. The average person may *think* this, but just like the guy who predicted Alf Landon's landslide in 1936, he's all wrong.

Ninety per cent of all our major automotive advancements in the past forty years were the direct developments of automobile racing. Nearly everyone knows that the rear view mirror was a "gadget" first used on an Indianapolis race car, and like the simple rear view mirror, just about every major part in use on today's automobiles is the direct outcome of a group of barnyard racing men. The list could start with Henry Ford the First who raced many times and broke records at Daytona Beach, putting his findings from this racing to use in the famous Model T. Eddie Rickenbacker, a former Indianapolis race driver and now president of Eastern Airlines, put his race knowledge to work when he built his own car, the Rickenbacker. Hydraulic brakes were first used on the Indianapolis track and were adapted by Rick in his car back in 1923. Jimmy Murphy, the first American to win a major Grand Prix in Europe, was the first to have four-wheel brakes on his race car. Modern fuels, suspension systems, shock absorbers, spark plugs, fuel pumps, disc and other type brakes now in use, were all first developed and first used on race tracks.

Modern tires for stock cars were improved as a result of race drivers' demands. In 1950, for instance, during the 500-mile Darlington, South Carolina, stock car race, there were 511 tire blow-outs. Seven years later, in 1957, there wasn't a *single* blow-out, even though the pace was much faster, and the distance the same. What happened was that the tire manufacturers just couldn't stand the pressure of thousands of people seeing their tires blowing-out at every turn, so they went to work with racing men and developed tires with some staying power and guts.

From a military viewpoint, the Jeeps and other four-wheel trucks and tractors all utilized the four-wheel drive developed by Harry Miller on an Indianapolis car. Fighting planes and PT boats borrowed the superchargers and intercoolers that were developed by Harry Miller and Augie Duesenberg on different race cars. The superchargers used on our World War Two fighters were basically the same as those designed for Miller's Indianapolis cars.

High-compression engines were first tried out on racetracks, as were light-metal pistons. Pressure cooling was a race track development, through Hitler's personal Mercedes racing team. Hitler's teams of Auto-Unions and Mercedes weren't just for sport, but to supply the military and Luftwaffe with tried engines and components of proven superiority. The fact that Hitler damn near beat the whole world with his advanced machinery was the direct result of knowledge gained on the automobile racing circuits. Oddly enough, the Germans admit this, but in America, where racing did the same for us, our Washington boys slip on their ostrich suits and bury their fat heads in the sand. Thank God, not all do this. Generals like the Air Force's LeMay and Griswold are both ardent racing fans who've spent many hours in the pits at LeMans with the writer. They realize the value of auto racing, and encourage the sport for the men under them. The 2000-hp Pratt & Whitney engines (heart of our famous P-47 fighter planes) would have been shot down like clay pigeons at a clambake if it hadn't been for the intercoolers Augie Duesenberg developed for his race cars. Today's rear axles, oil filters and pumps, and even gas lines, were first worked out on racing cars.

If racing were banned, as some legislators *are* trying to do, it would be like forbidding boys in college to study chemistry, or engineers to study physics. A much-used but little-appreciated well would be dried up. There has been some shouting that "racing should be banned because so many have been killed at it." Well, pure statistics prove that many more are killed each year in hunting accidents, or drowned while boating or swimming—why not ban these first? Why not banish football and boxing? These take a strong toll; percentagewise, mountain-climbing is a real dilly. The reason there haven't been more cries against these other sports is because even a child of ten would realize how damn silly it would be—but auto racing is in a different position; far too few people realize what it has done for us, which makes it the easiest ox to gore in a publicity-seeking congressional or senatorial move.

Why do so few know about racing's contributions? That's an easy one to answer, too. What would they do with all those nice little models in white coats you see in TV commercials or in double-page spreads in national magazines? It's much more impressive to the buying peasants if a major auto company can claim, "Out of our Engineering Center comes the totally new electronic whisk broom for cleaning spilled ashes" or, "Our new six headlight display . . ." (guaranteed to be as effective as a carbide bicycle lamp). The truth is that a big part of the American automobile business consists of hoodwinking the public into believing that the industry is really doing something important, when the fact is that 90% of their efforts are under the direct supervision of *cost* engineers.

As a professional automobile tester of many years' experience, who tests all the automobiles made in America at least once every year, let me assure you that nine times out of ten when they advertise that they've developed a "new" this or that, or "redesigned" some old component, and hang such words as "totally new concept" on it, it merely means they found a way to cheapen it up and build it for less, and with any luck and the help of God, it may not break down. This is not an attempt to be funny, but is an observation of what most of the shouting is usually all about in Detroit. Most of the "research" is based on how to make it for less, or, "How cheap can we make it and still have it go?"

While our domestic manufacturers were still engaged in competition (up until June, 1957) they built the best and most honest cars in their entire history. Now, out of competition on the race tracks of the country, their products have slipped badly, in many camps.

Automobile racing, aside from being a great spectator sport, is an essential part of our American way, if we are to keep from becoming a nation of pantywaists. Its value to every one of us is beyond possible estimate, and as Bill France, President of NASCAR, once said when someone remarked that racing should be banned, "No one has ever held a gun to a race driver's head and told him he must drive." By the same token, no spectator was ever dragged to the grandstand. I've known just about every top driver in the world for more than a quarter of a century, and it's my sincere belief that if there was a *charge* of 25 dollars for every driver to race, and no prize money whatsoever, if they could afford it, all the drivers I've known would race anyway.

As this goes to press there's a lot of rumbling about outlawing racing in the United States. Some feel there isn't a chance of anyone putting a thing such as this over. To these, let me remind you that as popular as auto racing is, drinking has always been at least twice as popular, and a group of creased-heads put Prohibition over—it stayed with us for many years.

16

The Round Table

IN A BOOK LIKE THIS, THERE ARE A NUMBER OF subjects that need kicking around, but don't really warrant a full chapter—so how about pulling up a chair and we'll bat the breeze about a lot of little thises and thatses?

A question I'm often asked by readers is, "How close have we come in this country to building a truly great sports car?" Actually, we've come a lot closer, more than once, than the dyed-in-the-wool Continental Iron fan would ever concede. For example, years ago Briggs Cunningham came within a whisker on two occasions of winning the LeMans race. Why he didn't has been a matter of much conjecture, but both times when he might have won, it wasn't because of equipment failure. I was in the Cunningham pits during both these events, and though some may disagree with me, I feel he lost through poor judgment and poor strategy.

Take 1952: the winning Mercedes averaged 96 and a fraction miles per hour for the 24-hour grind. Cunningham and Bill Spear finished in the money with an average speed of just over 92 mph. Another Cunningham, driven by John Fitch and George Rice, was knocked out by Cunningham's own crew when it came in for refueling while running in third place. The mechanics in charge, hearing a clatter on the restarting of the engine, felt the car had swallowed a valve and withdrew it from the race. A half hour later, when this same car was started up in the infield to be moved, the engine was perfect, and only then were red faces in order. They had falsely condemned a car of their own which was running in third place at the time, and which had only a stuck valve caused by the heat expansion during the stop for refueling! A shot of oil through the carburetor intake or even a little running might have easily freed this expensive entry which instead was knocked out by an expensive goof in judgment.

Now, back to the Cunningham car that continued and finished. Keep in mind the winning Mercedes finished with a mild 96 mph average—about all it was capable of doing. The Cunningham cars were shipped home to West Palm Beach. The car that had finished successfully raced several times in this country, and when it came time to go to LeMans the next year, this same car that had completed the 24 hours at 92 mph, with little more than an engine tune-up (not even an overhaul) went back to LeMans and finished third at an average speed of better than 102 mph! This was the car as it had run the year before—nothing had been added to it, and the engine hadn't even been torn down. One year later, it averaged more than ten mph faster, and more than six mph faster than the winning Mercedes of the year before. Since weather and track conditions both years were practically identical, on this I'll rest my case.

In '53, going back to this same Chrysler-powered

Cunningham car, John Fitch, who was driving it, was running right up with the leading Jaguar for many hours. His pit crew gave him constant signals to slow down and finally called him in to explain why he wasn't following orders. Fitch later told me that the pit crew was afraid the car couldn't stand the pace he was driving it, but that he felt he was in a better position to judge the condition of the car than the boys in the pit. He told me that constant checks on the oil temperature and water proved the big Chrysler engine was running as cool as an Eskimo's nose and under no extraordinary stress whatsoever. To this day John is haunted by the thought that he could have possibly won LeMans if he'd been left alone. On this point no one could be sure, but it's a lead pipe cinch this great car could have won the 1952 race.

A lot of cool sports car men, including some close to Chevrolet engineering, feel that if the Automobile Manufacturers' Association hadn't banned factory participation in competition, Corvette might have come near to dominating sports car racing. It may sound like heresy to some, but at a recent Nassau race, Ferrari and Maserati team men made the explosive statement that Corvette had the best sports car brakes in the world!

Lance Reventlow and his Scarabs (basically custom American jobs with Corvette engines and brakes) just about chased everything off American race courses in 1958, including the Lister-Jags which, until the Scarab's introduction, were almost unbeatable. The canny foreigners who years before had perhaps anticipated such a move, knowing American engines in cars such as the Scarab would someday prove hard to handle, then whipped the International Formula around, making Scarabs with Chevy engines as eligible for 1959 as the Anastasia Boys for a Charleston Cotillion. In America we just haven't built any hot engines as small as the three-liter formula, which is a little over 180 cubic inches. If Reventlow had built his Scarab two or three years sooner, he'd have had a way more than even chance of walking away with LeMans, but then the formula boom was lowered, almost outlawing American entries.

Reventlow went to Louis Meyer's nut-and-bolt house where Harry Miller engines (now known as "Offenhausers") have been successfully built for many years. As race men know, the Offenhauser engine hasn't been changed since the days of Cal Coolidge, and their specialty for years has been finishing first at Indianapolis. In 1954 Briggs Cunningham had an Offy engine built for an experimental car he ran at LeMans, and reportedly it was doing fairly well until they had a transmission failure. Reventlow went to Meyer-Drake with the same problem: "Build me a three-liter engine that will be adaptable to the slow-downs and dig-outs of sports car racing for my Scarabs." As this goes to press, his eventual success is unknown—but one thing is sure—the boys across the pond didn't want any truck with those Chevrolet-engined Scarabs. Will we ever win LeMans? The chances aren't too bright at this writing because rules are meant to be changed, and the boys who make the rules aren't on our team.

Road Racing

Road racing as we knew it in the past (meaning racing over closed public highways) is just about at an end, with the possible exception of LeMans. Crowd control is almost impossible in this country, and definitely impossible in Europe, or for that matter, Cuba, Mexico and other spots where enthusiasm has over-run the brim on too many occasions. As this is being readied for the press, many of the European drivers have shown a keener interest for high-speed track running such as at Monza,

Italy. The crowds, too, slightly weary of watching cars brake to an almost full stop, round a bend and go off again, not to be seen for many minutes at a time, have found the sight of magnificent machinery flying around high-banked turns at close to 200 mph a brand-new set of jollies. With the new Daytona International Speedway track now open, we have another circuit with a 200-mph potential, and since speed has always been the prime basic product of all racing, this brings speed at its best, even though some of the technical niceties of cornering, braking and steering may not enjoy the importance they once held.

My assistant, Jim McMichael, in trying to explain a sports car race to a neophyte, once made a sharp and steely observation about sports car courses in America. He said, "The formula for building most sports car courses today is to build a series of real lousy fourth-rate roads similar to the typical road of forty years ago. Then they find out who can get around this old-time circuit the fastest." In America on a 4,000-mile trip from Seattle to Key West, or from Canada to Mexico, today's tourist would never encounter roads as offbeat and badly designed as the typical artificial sports car road-race course.

As Jim further stated, "While the government is spending billions building better roads, sports car groups have spent quite a few millions on a counter road-building program, making lousy ones." True, in Europe even today the majority of the major roads are pretty crummy when compared with ours. If you do much Alpine travel or even runs from Paris to the Riviera, European suspension and handling in a car will prove a lot better than cruising the same route in a Cadillac. However, more and more sports car men are showing interest in high-speed circuits which will give them a chance to let their steeds out a few extra notches.

Pro vs. Amateur

The professional-versus-amateur pitch had the Sports Car Club of America on the verge of civil war late in 1958, with California threatening to secede from the Union. This situation has been eased, but then there shouldn't have been any tension in the first place. The stand of the S.C.C.A. was that this was "an amateur sport for amateurs, to be run and driven by amateurs." Now, the writer has been a member of the S.C.C.A. for a long time and I find it hard to believe that some high officers of this club haven't known for years that professionals have been driving in and winning many of their major events. The typical real amateur show is pretty bad theater, and usually only fun for the participants and their kiddies. Just as in golf, there are amateur divisions and professional divisions, and there's no reason why both shouldn't play on the same course in the major events that the paying crowd will really lay out their dough to see. There's no reason why talented amateurs can't run against real pros and still remain untinged. They can have their strictly amateur shows in addition to the Open events, and everyone should be happy; after all, in Europe, amateurs and pros have been driving against each other since the beginning.

Tuning for High Speed

As Director of the annual Daytona Beach Speed Trials, I know, but find it hard to believe, how few real solid automobile men realize that a different type of tuning is needed for a high-speed run. Many a sports car has run on the beach in a record attempt and missed its potential mark by many miles an hour, just because it was tuned wrong for high-speed running. For example, in a typical "Flying Mile" run at Daytona Beach, the cars usually get a full two-and-a-half miles to get up to speed before entering the one-mile trap. If the car is pulling the right gear (and most of them don't), the engine will be flat-out and slightly past maximum horsepower. Now, at this peak rpm running, no commercial distributors on the market have enough advancing properties to keep the engine correctly timed. Many distributors today have a combination governor and vacuum advance, and since at open throttle there's practically no vacuum in the manifold at all, there's no advancing from this point; in fact, on some types of distributors the timing will be several degrees later at 5000 rpm than it was at 3000. This is positively getting the horse on the wrong end of the wagon.

The easiest way to understand timing is to compare it with duck shooting. If a duck is flying hard at right angles to you, forty yards out, and you shoot *at* the duck, even with a magnum charge you'll miss him by several yards. The way to hit him is to aim several yards ahead so that your comparatively slow-moving shot and the crossing duck will reach the same point at the same time. Spark timing involves the same problem. The ideal time to have the fuel mixture fire in the cylinder is right at the point of top dead center when its explosive expansion will drive the piston down, getting the most possible energy out of the fuel charge. Where the duck factor comes in is that the mixture actually is rather slow in igniting, and there's quite a time lag between the spark occurring at the plug and the mixture igniting.

However, when an engine is turning 5000 rpm and more, the piston on its upward compression stroke is traveling at a fantastic rate of speed—the more rpm, the faster it travels. Spark timing comes in when the spark is aimed far enough ahead of the piston's reaching top dead center to cause the mixture to ignite at the exact instant when the most power can be squeezed out of the load. The faster the piston moves, just like the duck shooter, the further ahead the spark must be aimed. In other words, generally speaking, most successful speed-trial cars have their timing advanced anywhere between six and fifteen degrees ahead of the manufacturer's specifications.

This means, even with the highest-octane fuels, some signs of pinging at the start and a pretty poor-running engine until the car is moving close to 100 mph. When my Thunderbird once won the speed trials it was timed twelve degrees in advance of normal, ran horribly until it reached 4000 rpm, but kept right on going up to its peak of 6600 rpm, and beat everything in its class. At factory timing specifications the most that could be wrung out of this engine was 5700 rpm.

Some years ago, my MG won the speed trials at Daytona Beach and made the fastest time ever run by an MG by many miles an hour—the secret formula was timing. MG's high-speed tuning manual and factory representatives agreed that the MG Mark II engine should be set *at* top dead center, regardless. When a factory competition man tells you his timing can't be improved on for speed trials, his word usually should be relied on. The fact remained, however, that Jim McMichael (not working for me in those days) had a faster MG than mine, and was the defending Class Champ. McMichael and I made a trial run the day before the event and he had me by a good two or three miles an hour. So, disregarding all advice from the factory, I re-timed my engine about six degrees ahead, as I recall, and topped McMichael by about five mph. No MG on the beach has beaten my M'Gillicuddy's time to this writing.

By the same token, for the Standing-Start Mile (or

acceleration trials), the reverse tactics are quite often in order. An engine will usually get going quicker and with more power from a standstill with a slight retard in timing; so the amount of the timing for acceleration trials must be set with the length of the course in mind. For example, for a quarter-mile run with a typical family car or production sports car, a degree or two late in timing might be just the formula for acquiring the silverware. However, in a half-mile drag or full mile, such as you run at Daytona, this late timing would kill your chances, because many sports cars can get close to flat-out in a mile from a standstill, and most of the hot family-type cars that compete at Daytona will be pushing a full 120 mph or better at this mark. For a one mile acceleration run, the top engine set-up man will quite often set the timing only a degree or two in advance of normal so that he still has good acceleration and enough advanced timing to get going pretty fast before he crosses the wire. Timing for acceleration events is a matter to be decided on at the spot, with the weight and type of the car in mind.

Where most factory men fall down in advising correct rear-axle ratio for speed trials is in their over-estimation of the power their engines can develop in a two-way run. In other words, they might start the first run with a 15-mph wind at their backs (this is quite typical of Daytona), and when they turn around to come back they are bucking a 15 mph headwind. Under these conditions, even a car as powerful as a Chrysler 300 may show a difference of 10-12 mph between its two runs. You can usually tell the cars that were geared correctly, because even with a 20-mph wind there will rarely be more than a three-to-four-mile-an-hour difference between their runs.

I remember when one team of factory entries arrived at the beach expecting to average about 145 mph. The chief engineer of the factory, who was with the team, had the cars pulling 2.92 gears. He was advised by some who knew the beach that despite his power potential he'd never be able to pull that gear both ways successfully, since even the sand has about a 5 per cent drag. This make had an optional 3.31 gear and another optional 3.54. Either one of these gears were advised by the writer and others instead of the gear he'd chosen to run with. The chief engineer was adamant, though, saying he had enough power to pull that gear through ten inches of snow and still win out. One of his cars averaged 133 mph and the other averaged 131 mph, which upset the factory quite a bit. By special arrangement, the day after speed week was over, they took these same cars and installed the two optional gears, 3.31 and 3.54, and ran them again two ways through the measured mile. The car with the 3.31 gear averaged 148 mph with one run of 151 mph, and the car with the 3.54 gear averaged 146 mph, even though it ran out of rpm and went through the trap with its valves floating like a Goodyear blimp. Ninety-nine times out of a hundred, the gear that'll let you get up the most rpm is the one to run—although many Detroit engineers are still unconvinced of this. On one successful speed trial car I ran, I tried out *nine* optional rear axle ratios before getting the one I liked, and this one was for a heavy-duty station wagon doing semi-buswork. It proved to be the right cog, as it allowed me to get up to peak power and stay there.

A few other speed trial tips to keep in mind is that with really fast cars (and this could also mean the most streamlined sports car) a good wax job will eliminate much skin friction and could mean as much as two or three extra mph. In some cars with automatic transmissions such as Chryslers, pulling out some of the transmission oil (meaning half or more) will have the same effect as lightening the flywheel—this is especially helpful in acceleration trials. Fifty pounds of air in the tires at least is a must, except in some acceleration trials where an unfirm surface such as sand might call for less pressure in the rear (for traction), but fifty or more pounds in the front are needed under all competitive circumstances.

Injustice

One thing that has plagued many a sports car man is that, with the aid of some corny newspapers, just because he owns a sports car he is immediately suspect by the minions of the law. In many sections of the country a cracker-barrel cop would rather catch one sports car with a "dude" in it (as they say) than six family-type cars going twenty miles an hour faster. I know this is a pretty ridiculous situation, but the fact remains that it is true—certain cars are cop bait and certain cars aren't. I recall talking to a Georgia cop once who said, "Just love to catch those guys with the funny little hats in those sports cars." By the same token, I was pulled over just yakking with a turnpike cop once on a section of the pike that was zoned for 50 mph. A guy in a VW whipped by flat-out and doing a full 70 mph, and I looked at the cop. "Gonna pull him in?" I asked. "Not *me*," he smiled. "If I brought one of those in I'd be the laughing stock of the barracks."

On several occasions while cruising with two sports cars through the south on tests and watching all the speed limits and laws like hawks, we noticed that the moment small town cops spotted us they usually got on our tails and escorted us right through town to the outer "city limits"—obviously waiting for us to pull a single goof they could jump us for. I remember one time when I was running an American car through Georgia fast, right behind two sports cars wearing New York plates, all headed north. Mile after mile I trailed them; there wasn't a mile-an-hour difference between any of the three cars and we were all going about 10 mph over the limit. Out of nowhere a cop car whizzed by me, knocked off the two sports cars and never gave me a second look, even though we hadn't been separated by more than 150 yards for miles. Sure, it's injustice, but then the world's been loaded with injustices ever since Eve tossed Adam the fruit. There are some cars that can travel coast to coast year in and year out at 5-10 mph above the speed limit and never be touched. There are a lot of sports cars that'll be knocked off while still running under the speed limit. As a general rule-of-thumb, most small-town cops hate sports cars, and some curbstone judges are far from being in love with them, either.

Is There a Living in Sports Cars?

Another question readers often write in and ask is, "How much money can be made as a professional race driver, or in running a sports car agency?" Taking the first part first, there have been quite a number of men who've made fairly handsome livings (usually for a short time) as race drivers, but for every one of these, several dozen systematically starve. It's been said for a long time that a win at Indianapolis is worth a cool $100,000 to the driver, coming from endorsements, possible movie work, and the usual 40% of the purse, if he's not the car's owner (and very few are). On the stock car circuits, a handful of drivers have cleared better than $50,000 a year for several years running, and perhaps another handful better than $30,000. Beyond these—Siberia and destitution, or an existence of scrounging from one track to another, with doughnuts and coffee being a hearty meal.

In Europe, where the social standing of professional

drivers is several notches above that of all but a few American drivers, the professional Grand Prix man makes more than the typical European bank president. The top European drivers are quite often associated with factory teams at healthy salaries. In addition, they're allowed to seek out extra income from oil companies, tobacco, wine and whiskey interests, who pay high for endorsements. Bear in mind, in Europe the top Grand Prix drivers are, to the public, the same as our Mickey Mantles, National Open Golf Champs, or Heavyweight Title holders are to us. Racing is *the* major sport abroad. Drivers like Sterling Moss (who made the Queen's List in '58) have not only been honored as heroes, but in Moss' case, recognized by royalty to boot. There is a much better opportunity for a European to make a life's career out of driving than for an American, and the people are inclined to remember heroes longer than we are.

In any country, if you're the tops you'll make out well financially, and the meatballs will go on forever. A "meatball" in racing circles is generally considered the not-too-talented driver who, with mediocre equipment, enters every race (in many cases out of pure enthusiasm). He is the boy who fills in the field, and is a much-needed prop to make the heroes stand out. He creates the "lap traffic" for the hero in his superior equipment to whip through, and though his name will probably go unsung in all the record books aside from his mother's diary, without him there would rarely be any contests.

Take a big sports car race with 25 entries, let's say. If the event is typical, the field will contain three or four top drivers (always supplied with the best equipment, either from dealers or enthusiastic owners), which means the other 20 or 21 in the event will be props or spear-carriers, now known as "meatballs." The event is at best a three- or four-car event to start with. Rarely do the off-beats crash through with a win, unless the top boys all break down. Fortunately for racing, professional and amateur, at Indianapolis or LeMans, there is an unending supply of meatballs to make the events and wins look possibly more impressive than they are.

In the early days (meaning Vanderbilt Cup days) most of the entrants were either gentlemen drivers like Willie K. Vanderbilt or fierce-looking team men from Stuttgart or Paris. My very first ride was in a Mercedes team car driven by a German driver known as "Litchen." I was born in my family's house in New York City, and when the family decided to move out to the country for the summer, my transportation was a big 40-50 Mercedes with Litchen at the wheel. My father was then manager of Mercedes in this country. My first real ride with a going race driver was around Larchmont with Dario Resta in the car with which he won the 1916 Indianapolis race. Charlie Singer (who also built the Palmer-Singer car) was sponsoring Resta somehow, and the car was tried out around Larchmont before being shipped to Indianapolis. Our garage in Larchmont was the headquarters for the Mercedes Vanderbilt Cup team, and years later when we lost the house to the bank during the Great Depression, our garage was still jammed with tools and parts for old Mercedes. In fact, there was a complete Rolls-Royce chassis in the garage, belonging to me, that wouldn't have brought fifty dollars as junk—so everything was left there. What a field day I'd have with those parts today since the antique craze caught fire in the late 1940s!

Now that the first part of the original question has gotten so far off the track, let's tackle the second part: can you make enough dough with a foreign or sports car agency? The answer is "Yes, but probably not." It's quite similar to trying to make money playing "21" in Las

Vegas. Actually, the average sports car agency is very much like a country real estate office, meaning a supposed business, manned by incompetents. When I was a young sprout, if the average fairly well-to-do family had a male heir of no particular talent aside from laziness, and greatuncle Charlie didn't want him in his business, there were usually one or two outlets to keep him from appearing completely odd. One was to stick him in the insurance business selling policies, and the other was to get him a job as a real estate salesman.

The insurance part worked a little better for the agencies because they knew if they could get one of the rich boys in the town to work for them on a straight commission basis, he'd undoubtedly wangle his Aunt Nell's barn insurance, his mother and father's fire insurance, and old Uncle Proctor's yacht insurance. If he had enough relatives, it was a good thing for the agency who somehow managed to hold on to a fair percentage of such business long after Bufflehead decided to take his talents to other fields, having run out of sales the instant he ran out of family.

The real estate broker of the average suburban or country town (and even in New York City) was glad to get this type (naturally, on a commission basis) because they were handy, not only in answering the phone and taking messages, but in giving the office a slightly busier look when clients dropped in, and it was all for free. Now, in this second part of the twentieth century, foreign and imported car sales rooms have robbed many an insurance and real estate outfit of their former free help. There is just a bit more swashbuckle to demonstrating a Jag than in showing off the excellent closet space in Aunt Minnie's home to a prospective tenant of the agency. True, most of them don't make any more money, but still many an imported car lot is filled with free question-answerers who'll assure you on anything from the wheel-base of a Goggomobil to how to get a Ferrari in competition tune.

To get back to the question, "Can you make money in this business?" The answer is simple—hundreds do, and thousands don't. Many a man has made a successful career out of real estate and insurance, and some imported car dealers and salesmen have done very well; but the ones who have would have done well in many other fields, too, because they were basically good businessmen or good salesmen and weren't in the business just for the fun of playing store, as the others are. From a pure business standpoint, the mark-ups on the more popular imports are nothing for a real professional automobile man to get out of breath over. The percentage is rarely as high as that given by Detroit products; often a car salesman selling one Ford, Chevy or Plymouth will make as much as the import peddler selling two or three Volkswagens.

The Detroit dealer is quite often not only playing with a bigger profit percentage, but has a more expensive car to sell, backed by millions of dollars in advertising to help him. Also, if the import dealer is working with a real hot number, such as the VW, he can't get enough cars to fill his orders. This is heartening in one way, but it hardly pays the rent. Many domestic-make dealers have taken on the sale of imports, and you may see such uncommon bedfellows as Lincoln-Mercury and SAAB, or Ford and Volvo under the same roof. They've taken these imports on, in most cases, to help pay for the bare overhead which, even with popular models, can rarely be done. The out-and-out import dealer has a much harder row to hoe. Though it has been done successfully, it wasn't easy, and took real top men to do it. In the first place, he must get volume and he must have a car (sports or economy sedan) that is well-known today, popular and salable. If he has to educate each customer on the virtues of his product, he has a lap-full of trouble, even though the product he's pushing is of Tiffany-diamond quality.

Service, which is very profitable to some foreign car shops, is a major headache to others, because getting good mechanics with foreign car knowledge is just slightly less difficult than reaching the men's finals at Forest Hills with a broken leg. In fact, the life of many an agency hangs on its mechanics for its very existence. In the average community if the owner of an import is kept happy, he will, through his enthusiasm, make a lot of sales for that agency. On the other hand, one word at the country club by an owner that he has to take his Jackalap Six to New York for service because the local agency is "no damned good" and the chances are a half-dozen sales will be hung on the hook right there.

To enter the sports or foreign car business successfully, a man should first be assured of his capital and, after that, he should be assured of service help, location and type of cars, their availability and salability. He should have a pretty accurate knowledge beforehand on what percentage of income he can expect from service and how much from sales. He must bear in mind if he sells a car like the VW, service doesn't amount to enough to keep one mouse in cheese for the first 30,000 miles. He must also bear in mind his proximity to the nearest parts depot, because nothing discourages a foreign car buyer quicker than having to wait two weeks for a valve lifter or timing gear. By the same token, an ample parts supply on hand for the more expensive imports can run into an investment large enough to choke a Sultan.

The prettiest part of the import picture in a thriving community that is gold on the surface (and sometimes low-grade iron underneath) is that you can usually get a franchise without busting the vaults of the local bank. A good Ford or Chevy dealership is an expensive piece of property in any worthwhile area and can easily cost from a quarter of a million to a million, or more, to buy. The import dealer is rarely faced with an initial nut like this, and his used car problem will rarely get to the choking point it can with the big American dealerships. There is money being made in sports car dealerships by the smart hard-headed business boys who put business first and the gung-ho part of the product a late twelfth. The type of agency that is founded on the owner and his pals having a lot of fancy cars to run around in usually lasts until junior runs out of dough or Aunt Nell announces she's had it. It's a business for professionals, and only fun for a while for the kiddies.

In the good old days you've heard Gramp talk about, an import salesman could really make himself a wad of dough if he had a few good clients—a condition that just doesn't exist today. It was possible for a salesman to make as high as two or three thousand dollars on a single sale of a special-bodied Mercedes, Isotta or Hisso back in the 1920s. It was possible for the dealer to make as much as six or seven thousand dollars on a single sale—the full price of a Fleetwood Cadillac today. Those were the gravy days in the import business. I had one pal who lived in the New York Athletic Club and who had three clients and didn't bother with any more. These three clients were big families who always bought the most expensive imports. My pal never saw the year he made less than $15,000 in those days (which was like $30,000 today), and it took up very little of his time. *They* called *him* when they wanted to buy, and he had a deal on with all the top import agencies who knew him and his clients—so he was in a position to sell them any make they might want.

As far as service was concerned in those days, it was a robber's haven. Many top garages had clients that brought in their big imports once a year for a general going-over (which merely meant a tune-up, occasionally a valve job and brakes, and once in a long while rings). The standard fee was $1,200, regardless. Cleaning out the carburetor on a Silver Ghost Rolls-Royce really meant unsnapping the clevis pin and yanking out the governing piston and wiping off the gum. It cost twenty-five bucks in every reputable shop from coast to coast, and was a hard three minute's work for a slow mechanic and absolutely no tools, not even a screwdriver, were needed. The average Silver Ghost was good for about six of these a year. Smart owners who read the manual did this themselves. A lot of owners asked for it, though.

On occasions it was fun to be a thief. I remember one time in my shop when a well-known South American playboy stormed in and accusingly told us he wasn't going to be robbed. I'd never seen the man in my life before, and neither had any of my crew. This took place in my Palm Beach shop. When we finally got him calmed down we learned that his $20,000 beauty was lying dead in the road about two miles from my shop. Before he would even let us go out to look at it, however, he told me he knew exactly what it would cost to fix it ($265) and exactly what was wrong, as it had happened twice before. He said, "the ring gear has sheared its teeth, and the car is immobile." He was so generally disagreeable that I was about to throw him out of the shop, but my curiosity got the better of me. When he asked how long it would take to get parts from New York (he knew *we* wouldn't have them in Florida) I told him, "About four days." He then announced, "If you'll do the job for $265.00 and throw in the towing charge, you can go ahead—otherwise I'll get someone else." I told him no soap, not until I'd looked at it, but I'd tow it in for free, and to phone me back in a couple of hours. He agreed, called a taxi and stormed off.

When we got his big blunderbuss into the shop it took less than a minute to discover the trouble. There were six bolts, worth about a cent and a half apiece, that connected the drive shaft to the rear axle; these bolts had sheared. I sometimes wonder if they'd been set up loose on purpose, as he'd told me the name of the well-known New York shop (still in business today) that had done the "$265 job" twice before. We could have fixed the car like new in five minutes, but my surly customer had asked for it just a little too hard, and in those days I was the boy to give it to him. His car was jacked up and put on blocks. When my rude customer phoned, I told him he was right and we'd fix it for $265. The car stayed on the blocks for five days, and the owner came in and inspected it several times. The end of the fifth day we replaced the bolts, our South American boy paid like a major, and I guess both of us were very happy about the whole thing. A thief?—sure, but not without provocation. . . . Those were the days.

17

What It's All About

BY THE TIME YOU GET TO THIS CHAPTER, YOU ARE probably sold or unsold forever on sports, competition, or rally-type cars, as against typical, no-talent Detroit balloons. You may realize that the people who buy these off-beat vehicles are mostly non-conformists who couldn't care less what Mrs. Pottsybelly up the street thinks, or, for that matter, the entire Board of Directors of the General Motors Corporation. The one thing nearly all sports car and rally car men have in common is a resentment against regimentation that dictates not only how they must live, but what they must go through life in. As we wrote in *The Modern Sports Car* back in 1954, unless you have the "feel," sports cars are definitely not for you. The man who doesn't "feel" that his MG, Austin-Healy, or Jaguar is a sporting and adventure companion, just doesn't have it. Let's take an imaginary case.

It's quarter past two, you're having lunch at the Forum with your fellow junior partner, Charlie, and Old

Man Hasinger, of Philadelphia Tool & Die. Your advertising firm has handled Hasinger's account for years—a steady, but not over-lucrative account. Philadelphia Tool, with it's relatively small two-million-dollar advertising budget, is nice institutional stuff, and though you're the account executive, it isn't the big-time stuff you dreamed of, though it's steady and Hasinger's a helluva nice guy.

The check paid, you are lazing over your extra coffee when Hasinger asks, "Say, isn't that Keenan Wynn over there at the second table?" As it turns out, it is. Then Hasinger tells you, "Why, only last night we saw a re-run of that old TV play Wynn did called 'The Sport'—terrific show," Hasinger continues, "It's about a meek little guy, set in his ways like cement, who drives a car like everyone else in the neighborhood and has the same kind of wife. It seems this meek little guy going no place fast busts out of the traces one day and buys one of these little foreign sports cars. His wife thinks he's crazy, his domineering boss thinks he's a lunatic, and it looks pretty dark for The Sport, who says 'to hell with them.' Then things begin to pick up all over for him. When he goes to pick up the firm's most important client, he does it in his sports car, and when the boss learns this he almost fires The Sport on the spot. It all turns out OK, because the big client thinks the sports car is great, and Wynn's great, so Wynn ends up a partner in the firm or something—all because he bought that funny little sports car. Anyway, Keenan Wynn was real great and it was one of the funniest shows I've ever seen on television," Hasinger concludes.

You'd seen this show on TV yourself, but you don't let Hasinger know. That night, when you have some time alone, you start reviewing the day and yourself. You're 38, have been with Mixture & Sells for thirteen years, making a good salary, but haven't done much stirring on the ladder rungs in quite some time. In fact, old J. B. has been taking you for granted for several years and you are beginning to feel like one of the wall fixtures in the office. As a matter of fact old J. B. hasn't asked you to go after a big account for nearly two years. Jack Riper is the pet new-business man of the firm, and his consistent-in-the-70s golf and membership in three top clubs doesn't hurt him a bit.

"You're in just a good old-fashioned rut, boy," you tell yourself, "like the temperature in a deep salt mine—never too hot, never too cold." "Sort of a renewal order clerk," you feel, "keeping the old small boys like Hasinger happy, and leaving the big plums to Jack."

The picture you are drawing of yourself isn't too pretty—just a steady ride to rigor mortis. You begin thinking about Hasinger—lunch and his tale about "The Sport"—"You know," you say to yourself, "that 'Sport' story could fit a lot of guys like me. Here I am, 38, married to a gal who takes me for granted, just as the boss does. I own a new Cadillac four-door sedan, have a seven-room apartment on East 72nd Street, take a two week's vacation every summer in Nantucket, and that about sums it up. I drink my share of martinis, go to the theater occasionally, and Morocco now and then with some of the boss' choicer clients. Guess I'm a pretty dull bastard. When I was a kid in college I was a fair athlete, liked sailing and swimming, and even owned a hopped-up Ford with two carburetors and dual exhausts. Gee, that car was a lot of fun."

You let your thoughts wander, but they float listlessly in a sullen sky. Hell, you even had a dog in the old days—you haven't owned a dog in 15 years, and you *like* dogs. Your mind goes back to "The Sport."

The next night when you are hailing a cab in front

of the office on the way home, only to have two nabbed right out from under you, you think, "To hell with it, I'll walk home, haven't done that in years." You find yourself strolling up Park Avenue and tell yourself you're not doing it on purpose, but you know damn well you are. You could have crossed over at 49th Street, but no, the first showroom is still on your side, so you keep going just as if being drawn by a magnet—you're there. You look in the windows—they sure don't look like your Cadillac, and you see yourself tooling down some country lane behind the wheel of one of these. The stoop automatically goes out of your shoulders and you can feel your muscles toning up, just from the mental picture. You're strong though, so you don't go in, but go across the street.

There's a red 300SL Mercedes in that window, and you can almost feel water gathering up in your mouth. However, you're an intelligent man, so you flag a cab and go home. Three nights later you are deliberately back in front of that window, viewing the Mercedes. You go in, feeling like a man about to meet his maker. This Lorelei of the Rhine country is singing a siren song that bursts your eardrums from within. You try the seat—God! what comfort—never felt any car like this; you look at the material of the convertible top—you step out and look at the finish and the paint, and then you ask, "How much?" Your knees buckle slightly and you tell the salesman, "I'll think it over," and you leave.

That night you're penciling on an envelope. "Let's say I could sell the Caddy for $4,000—still leaves me a little over $6,500 short. $2,200 bucks worth of Government bonds—guess I could raise the balance at the bank. Your trained better sense, resulting from years of experience, takes over. "Don't be an idiot—tear up the envelope and forget the whole thing."

The next afternoon you excuse yourself from the

office for an hour, and Mr. Warren at the bank says "Certainly." Three of the longest nights of your life later you tell your wife after dinner, "I've got to put the car in the garage—I had it out today. It's downstairs."

"Why don't you just call the garage and tell them to pick it up, the way you always do?" she answers.

You tell her no, in the future you're always going to drive it over yourself—the garage boys might wreck it. She looks at you strangely, but then, she'd been doing that for years.

"You've got to come down with me tonight," you tell her, "I have a surprise for you."

She shrugs, and says, "Wait till I get my coat." You lead her through the long foyer, down the elevator, out the door, and there it is! alongside the curb.

"Where is our car parked?" she asks. You tighten the grip on her arm and steer her right to the Teutonic red beauty.

"What's this?" she asks.

"It's ours, dear, all signed up and paid for."

She steps back. "Where is our Cadillac?" she demands.

"I traded it in on this" you tell her.

"You must have lost your mind" she almost screams, whirls on her toe and stomps back into the apartment.

It's Saturday before she'll take another look. You never mention the price to her, and as you both start on a drive to the country, she does concede that the seats are comfortable and it is rather pretty, "in a childish sort of way." When the doorman at the country club spies you and exclaims "Boy, what a car!" the wife starts to perk up just a bit. When you are leaving and old Mr. Simmons asks, "Is that yours?" and then adds "gorgeous," your wife looks more amenable than she has in some time.

In fact, she now tells her friends, when they call,

about the new Mercedes, and when Ethel Betz says "My, the advertising business must be doing very well," she asks later that night, "Just how much did it cost?" You lie as you haven't lied in years. You tell her about a deal and make innuendos about "wholesale prices" etc. You are undoubtedly thoroughly unconvincing, but you don't tell.

Now comes February, and Philadelphia Tool & Die is having its annual sales and promotion meeting in Palm Beach. Just a few key men attend, but since you are the account executive, it's good business to be there. You plan to fly down, spend a few days, then fly back. New York is fogbound—you phone Washington—that's socked in, too. Trains have been booked for weeks. Suddenly it hits you—I could drive down there easily in two days—how about it? You hastily pack, kiss your wife goodbye and head for the garage. "What a grind" you feel.

Four hours later you've been through New Jersey, part of Delaware, across Maryland's Eastern Shore and are going over the Chesapeake Bay Bridge. That night you hole up in Raleigh, North Carolina. Amazingly enough you're not tired. You've had so much fun getting to know your new pal, the big Mercedes, that the time has just flown. You'd forgotten how a car should handle in this fog—not since the days of your hopped-up Ford have you had so many thrills on the road. And the way this baby takes the corners without squealing or leaning soon has you driving with an almost permanently set smile. "By God, this is fun" you tell yourself as you whizz along. "Too bad so many people don't know about it."

The next afternoon you're entering Florida, and just as darkness sets in you pull into Daytona Beach. You'd made a five A.M. start, and this time you are tired, but boy, what fun. You could go on, but why? The meeting doesn't start until tomorrow night. You notice two other

300SLs like yours and several other sports cars with out-of-state licenses parked at the restaurant. As you get out a young kid in an Austin-Healey asks "Gonna run that in the speed trials?" You tell him "No" but then the kid continues, "Boy, I sure would if I had a car like that." At dinner, the kid is at the next table with a girl, and he introduces you to several other people passing by as "This is the guy who owns that red 300SL outside—it's a real gasser." The first thing you know, several people are sitting at your table asking if you're going to run at Sebring or at the Daytona track. When you tell all of them "No," you can literally see your stock dropping in the eyes of the askers.

The next night in Palm Beach you tell old man Hasinger about how his story got you to be a "Sport" too. He and several others come outside to look "it" over, with mixed enthusiasm. "Gonna run it at Daytona Beach?" Hasinger asks, you are about to say no when that seventh sense that all good account men have tells you to reply, "Maybe." Hasinger won't let it go at this, saying, "I'd like to see those trials myself, maybe I'll go up with you." Just as you're getting ready to say goodnight to Hasinger he tells you, "Tomorrow we'll spend the day deep-sea fishing. Some of the boys don't like it, so there'll just be Fred Coatesworth, myself and Ed Badley—want to come along?"

The name "Fred Coatesworth," hits you right between the eyes. He, who until then you never knew was a pal of Hasingers', is Chairman of the Board of Raven Cosmetics, just about the biggest advertising account in the field, and one that Jack Riper has been trying to collar for over two years. You answer, "Yes, I'd love to go." And when you get back to the hotel bar alone for a goodnight drink, you begin to recall a lot of things that took place at Mixture & Sells policy meetings.

You remember the time when old JB asked Jack if he

was making any progress in trying to get some business from Raven, and Jack answered, "Not an inch. Old Man Coatesworth swings the whole deal himself, and it would take a subpoena from the Senate to reach him." Well, anyway, even if Coatesworth doesn't afford you a second look on the fishing trip, the fun you'll get out of telling Jack Riper you spent the day with him should prove a real ball. You smile to yourself, thinking how Riper would rip you up for not making the most of such an opportunity.

It is just after eight o'clock when Hasinger slips into the passenger seat alongside of you, and you head for Lew Parkinson's Sailfish Center. As you pull into the parking lot, Hasinger shouts, "Hey, you old mossback" to a man just emerging from a 150S Jaguar. The man wheels and eyes the 300SL and shouts back at Hasinger, "Well, what in hell are you doing in that? . . . What a car!"

You are introduced to Coatesworth, who asks if you'd mind his trying the front seat. He slips behind the wheel. "Boy this is what I want," he exclaims, "But Nelly would kill me for sure—she still thinks I'm in my second childhood for buying this Jag." A moment later the hood is up and Coatesworth's rapid-fire line of adulation is streaming forth. Lew Parkinson comes up and says "You fellows interested in fish?" The incident is over.

It is one of those rare days of the Gulf Stream—sort of oily and hot, and before an hour has passed, Coatesworth has hooked and boated a sizeable white marlin. This is a phenomenon in itself, since it is a little early for the Marlin to be this far north. Some two hours later Coatesworth again gets a strike on a 7-foot sail. It is brought alongside, tagged and released. After that, things slow a bit, when Coatesworth asks you what you do. When you tell him you're with Mixture & Sells he says, "Yes, I know the firm and have considered several times giving them some business." "Can always use it," you laughingly retort, and the conversation stops as Old Hasinger hooks into a good sized King.

Back at the dock that evening, Coatesworth asks, "You gonna race that at Sebring or Daytona?" You know better than to give such a car enthusiast a flat "No," but answer, "Afraid I'll have to get back to work, I'm due in New York Monday." Back at the cars, Coatesworth again says, "Boy, I love that car, do you think I'd be a fool to buy one?"

From somewhere in the Great Beyond your late grandfather, who used to be a card sharp on a riverboat, must have whispered to you to toss in your ace. This is the hardest instant decision you ever had to make, because you now think as much of that red Mercedes as you do of your wife, and there are some things you just don't lend. "Mr. Coatesworth," you say, "I'm going to be in town for another two days—here are the keys—take it and I'll take your car. This will give you a chance to make up your mind."

He jumps at this like a mongoose after a cobra, you brief him on the starting switch and instruments and then say "Have fun, Mr. Coatesworth," which he answers with, "Call me Fred."

The next afternoon Coatesworth is at your hotel saying, "I'm sold, I just ordered one. Here are your keys." And as Coatesworth is about to depart, he turns and says "Could you meet me at '21' for lunch next Tuesday? I've some business you could handle for me, if you're interested."

When you get back to Daytona, you are tempted to drive over to the beach and maybe give the speed trials a run, but then something tells you not to press your luck, and you keep heading north.

Tuesday afternoon, on your return from lunch with a sizable hunk of Raven business in your inside pocket, old J. B. is almost speechless, and Jack Riper is visibly felled, but he quickly regains himself to say, "I'll start working on a campaign for them immediately." You smile and then remind him right in front of J. B., "Thanks, Jack, but this is my account, and Fred wants me to handle it *my* way."

That extra-large bonus J. B. hands you six weeks later is way more than the original investment in the big Mercedes, but you can't help laughing when he tells you: "You know the Ames Steel Account Jack's been working on for over a year? I wish you'd give it a try. You might drive out and see old man Ames at Southhampton some weekend, but, and I mean no offense, maybe it would be better if you didn't go out in that silly little car I hear you're driving. Big company men don't think too much of that sort of thing."

On the drive down to Southhampton your mind goes to that kid in the Austin-Healey at Daytona. You begin to think you might like to try the speed trials or even a small non-professional race. It'd be fun—wonder what J. B. would say about that?

This could have happened—in fact, it did—only the names were changed to protect the innocent. Since Julius Caesar's day, leaders in any field use the common man to fill their ranks, and put the rarer, non-conformist thinkers in charge. This formula is no guarantee that it'll make you a million dollars, but it is a guarantee that if you've been leading a staid little life in a staid little way, a good sports car may put some of the hair back on your chest and get you a name, not a serial number.

Index

D